THE FLINTSTONES™ COLLECTIBLES

AN UNAUTHORIZED GUIDE

Debra S. Braun

Schiffer® Publishing Ltd
4880 Lower Valley Road, Atglen, PA 19310 USA

DISCLAIMER

The Flintstones™ is a registered trademark of Hanna-Barbera Productions, Inc. All pictures, graphics, and photos compiled herein are intended to heighten the awareness of The Flintstones™ and related products. This book is in no way intended to infringe on the intellectual property rights of any party. All products, brands, characters, and names represented are trademarks or registered trademarks of their respective companies.

The information in this book was derived from the author's independent research and was not authorized, furnished, or approved by Hanna-Barbera Productions, Inc.

Library of Congress Catalog Card Number: 99-66311

Designed by "Sue"
Type set in Lithograph/Korinna BT

ISBN: 0-7643-1017-8
Printed in China
1 2 3 4

Published by Schiffer Publishing Ltd.
4880 Lower Valley Road
Atglen, PA 19310
Phone: (610) 593-1777; Fax: (610) 593-2002
E-mail: Schifferbk@aol.com
Please visit our web site catalog at
www.schifferbooks.com

This book may be purchased from the publisher.
Include $3.95 for shipping.
Please try your bookstore first.
We are interested in hearing from authors
with book ideas on related subjects.
You may write for a free catalog.

In Europe, Schiffer books are distributed by
Bushwood Books
6 Marksbury Ave.
Kew Gardens
Surrey TW9 4JF England
Phone: 44 (0)208 392-8585; Fax: 44 (0)208 392-9876
E-mail: Bushwd@aol.com
Free postage in the UK. Europe: air mail at cost.
Try your bookstore first.

CONTENTS

Lunch box, metal. Aladdin Industries Inc., 1962. The Flintstones and Rubbles are shown watching a dinosaur school bus. Caption: "The Flintstones and Dino." Lunch box: 8.25" tall. $190-205. Thermos: 6.5" tall. $55-70.

DEDICATION

This book is dedicated to people who have rocks in their heads.

ACKNOWLEDGMENTS

I would like to extend a special thanks to my parents, Mark Coté, Peter and Nancy Schiffer, Jennifer Lindbeck, Tracey Curry, and the staff at Wink One Hour Photo. All of these people were instrumental in the development of this book. I really appreciate all of their guidance and support.

I would also like to thank my co-workers and friends for believing in me and making me smile.

Photography by: TOBY

INTRODUCTION

Bill Hanna and Joe Barbera met in 1939 at the Metro-Goldwyn-Mayer (MGM) animation studio. They worked together at MGM until 1957 when the animation division was eliminated. Soon after, Hanna and Barbera formed a partnership and created their own animation studio. They recruited many talented artists, narrators, and writers to work for them.

In the beginning, The Flintstones went through many stages until they were deemed a modern family living in the Stone Age. In fact, they were originally designed to be either hillbillies or pilgrims. Once the scene was set for Bedrock in 10,000 B.C., the story lines were infinitive.

On September 30, 1960, The Flintstones, written by Hanna and Barbera, debuted on primetime ABC. The show was an overnight success. After the first episode was aired, Warren Foster prepared scripts and storyboards for the next sixteen half-hour shows. The sitcom revolved around The Flintstones, the Rubbles, and their prehistoric pets. Each episode was so innovative and quick-witted that it was "pre-hysterical!" Watching The Flintstones soon became a Friday night tradition.

During the 1962-63 seasons, Wilma became pregnant. In February 1963, Pebbles was born in Room 12 of the maternity ward at the Bedrock hospital. She weighed 6 lbs. and 12 ozs., and is the first cartoon baby to have had a televised birth. During the episode, Barney suggests the name "Pebbles," because she is a chip off of a "Flint***stone***." A Pebbles doll was manufactured by Ideal in 1963 to commemorate the occasion, which returned an estimated $20 million in revenue.

After Pebbles was born, super strength Bamm-Bamm was adopted by the Rubbles. It is interesting to note that the story line of the show changed after the children were introduced, from one of light-hearted, prehistoric merriment to the candid trials and tribulations of parenting.

The Flintstones animated TV series ran from 1960-1966 and is one of the longest running on primetime television. Due to unpredictable ratings, The Flintstones were dropped from the ABC primetime lineup during their final season. At that time, NBC decided to pick up the series so that it could be aired on Saturday mornings.

Over the years, Hanna-Barbera Productions created over 3,500 half-hour animated programs. Approximately 195 of these half-hour episodes were dedicated to The Flintstones. In conjunction with television sitcoms, The Flintstones were transformed into comic books, comic strips, and collectible merchandise. All in all, there have been close to 3,000 licensed products produced. This Bedrock-based memorabilia continues to be collected by The Flintstones enthusiasts everywhere.

Even after 30 years, The Flintstones phenomena remains strong. Their show continues to have universal appeal and can be found translated into many different languages around the world. The secret to their long-lived success is that we can all relate to them. Their escapades mimic our everyday lives. I mean, haven't we all worked for a boss like "Mr. Slate," or had a best friend like "Barney?"

If you would like to write to the creators of The Flintstones, their address is as follows:

Hanna-Barbera Productions, Incorporated
3400 Cahuenga Boulevard
Hollywood, California 90068-1376

HELPFUL HINTS

Searching for The Flintstones items at toy shows, flea markets, and garage sales is challenging and fun. You never know what you are going to find. It is important to understand that the prices for The Flintstones memorabilia will fluctuate according to their condition, supply, and demand. You should purchase an object because you like it, not for an investment. This book is intended to heighten your awareness of The Flintstones collectibles and their approximate values in excellent to mint condition on a secondary market. All of the items shown in this book were produced between 1960 and 1999.

There are several things to consider before purchasing an object. For example: Is it in good condition? Are all of the pieces complete? Is it rare or hard to find?

It is my recommendation to inspect each item thoroughly. Especially look for chips, hairline cracks, paint peeling, and crazing in ceramic items.

Tip 1

One way to identify a hairline crack in an object is to hold it up to a light. The hairline crack should stick out instantly even if it has been repaired.

Tip 2

To feel a chip easily, gently move your finger around the entire surface of an object.

Tip 3

Price tags sometimes get so sticky that they can ruin any object. If you are considering to make a purchase, you may want to ask the vendor to carefully remove his price tag so that the exact condition is disclosed.

Tip 4

Sunlight can cause **permanent** discoloration to plastic or plush materials if an object is exposed over a significant period of time.

Tip 5

If an item is made up of multiple parts, take the time to make sure all pieces are accounted for. There is nothing more disappointing then putting together a puzzle that has pieces missing.

Tip 6

Before you purchase a battery-operated toy, check inside the battery compartment for corrosion. Also, you may want to carry an assortment of batteries to make sure the toy works.

> *Keep in mind that if a slight imperfection is in an inconspicuous place, then the object may still look nice on a display.*

Most of us are on a budget, so every penny counts. Once you have established what type of condition the object is in, you should also estimate a fair price. Lately, it appears that ceramic items in particular are commanding extremely high prices. I usually rate the object first on rarity, then on condition. If an object is rare, I would probably buy it at any price even with slight imperfections. However, if an object is common, I may wait until I can find it somewhere in mint condition.

I estimate the condition of an object on a scale from 1 to 10 and price it accordingly.

See the chart at the top of the next page.

One last thing, vendors at flea markets and toy shows **expect** you to barter on prices. Don't be shy! If an object is priced too expensive for the condition that it is in, let the vendor know in a diplomatic manner. If your criticism is warranted, the vendor will often reduce his asking price. *Best of luck in your hunting endeavors!*

Grade	Condition	Definition	Price example
1-4	Poor	Item shows major signs of wear. No tags and/or packaging present, i.e., noticeably broken, reglued, or discolored.	$1.00-$4.00
5	Fair	Item shows minor signs of wear and has some missing components. No tags and/or packaging present, i.e., missing puzzle or game pieces.	$5.00
6	Good	Item has been used and shows minor signs of wear. No tags and/or packaging present, i.e., small chip in an inconspicuous area or very slight crazing.	$6.00
7	Very Good	Item has been used but is still pristine. No tags and/or packaging present.	$7.00
8	Excellent	Item has been gently used but is still pristine. Original tags and/or packaging may be ripped or damaged.	$8.00
9	Near Mint	Item has been gently used but is still pristine. Original tags and/or packaging may be unsealed and slightly worn.	$9.00
10	Mint	Item has never been used and is pristine. Original tags are present and/or packaging is sealed from the factory.	$10.00

CHAPTER 1

FIGURINES

Figurines, plastic. Marx, N/A. Barney, Betty, Wilma, and Fred are shown standing on green bases. Under 1.5" tall. $10-15 each.

Figurines, plastic. Imperial, 1976. Fred, Wilma, Betty, and Barney. Under 3" tall. $10-15 each.

Figurines, rubber. Manufacturer unknown, N/A. Wilma with Pebbles, Fred, and Barney. Under 3.5" tall. $5-10 each.

Figurine, plastic. Kinder, 1994. Germany. Figurines were placed sporadically within chocolate eggs. Two versions of Fred were produced with either a dinosaur or lawn mower. Under 2" tall. $10-15.

Author's note: Kinder figurines are finely engineered. They are made up of small pieces that are put together like a puzzle. Early figurines have sticker eyes and accents; while later ones have painted features.

Figurine, plastic. Kinder, 1994. Germany. Betty. Under 2" tall. $10-15.

Figurine, plastic. Kinder, 1994. Germany. Two versions of Barney were produced with either a fishing rod or guitar. Under 2" tall. $10-15.

Figurine, plastic. Kinder, 1994. Germany. Wilma is shown holding a purse. Under 2" tall. $10-15.

Figurine, plastic. Kinder, 1994. Germany. Dino is shown standing on four legs. Under 2" tall. $15-20.

Figurine, plastic. Kinder, 1994. Germany. Dino is shown sitting up. Under 2" tall. $15-20.

Figurines, plastic. Frigee-Werk, 1996. Germany. Dino, Pebbles, Wilma, and Fred. Under 2" tall. $5-10 each.

Figurines, plastic. Frigee-Werk, 1996. Germany. Barney, Betty, and Bamm-Bamm. Under 2" tall. $5-10 each.

Figurine, plastic. Manufacturer unknown, 1991. Cereal premium. "Bedrock Bendable" series. Fred is shown holding a microphone. 3.75" tall. $5-10.

Figurine, plastic. Manufacturer unknown, 1991. Cereal premium. "Bedrock Bendable" series. Dino is shown playing drums with a pair of bones. 3.75" tall. $10-15.

Figurine, plastic. Manufacturer unknown, 1991. Cereal premium. "Bedrock Bendable" series. Barney is shown playing a guitar. 3.5" tall. $5-10.

Figurine, plastic. Manufacturer unknown, 1992. Cereal premium. "Hollyrock" series. Fred is shown holding a megaphone. Caption: "Director." 4" tall. $5-10.

Figurine, plastic. Manufacturer unknown, 1992. Cereal premium. "Hollyrock" series. Barney is shown holding a movie camera. Caption: "Hollyrock." 3.25" tall. $5-10.

Figurines, plastic. Manufacturer unknown, 1992. Cereal premium. An example is shown of the yellow boxes that were originally attached to the top of each cereal box.

Figurine, plastic. Manufacturer unknown, 1992. Cereal premium. "Hollyrock" series. Dino is shown holding a clipboard. Caption: "Take 1." 4" tall. $10-15.

Figurines, plastic. Manufacturer unknown, 1990. Cereal premium. Fred is shown holding a life preserver. Barney is shown holding a beach ball. Under 4.25" tall. $5-10 each.

Figurine, plastic. Manufacturer unknown, 1990. Cereal premium. A solid color Fred is shown holding a life preserver. 2.75" tall. $5-10.

Figurines, plastic. Manufacturer unknown, 1990. Cereal premium. Brontosaurus and Mammoth. Glow-in-the-dark. Under 1.5" tall. $5-10 each.

Figurines, plastic. Manufacturer unknown, 1991. Cereal premium. Dino is shown skiing and roller skating. Under 2.75" tall. $10-15 each.

Figurines, plastic. Manufacturer unknown, 1992. Cereal premium. Brontosaurus and Mammoth. Under 2.5" tall. $5-10 each.

Figurine, plastic. Manufacturer unknown, 1992. Cereal premium. Stegosaurus. 2" tall. $5-10.

Figurine, rubber. Manufacturer unknown, N/A. Cereal premium. Hoppy. 2.5" tall. $10-15.

Figurines, plastic. Manufacturer unknown, 1987. Cereal premium. Barney, Dino, and Fred. Under 2" tall. $5-10 each.

Figurine, metal. Vanity Fair Ind., Inc., 1977. Fred is shown holding a purple lunch box. His arms move up and down. 2.75" tall. $20-35.

Figurine, pewter. Colonial Pewter, 1980. King's Dominion. Fred. 1.75" tall. $15-20.

Figurine, pewter. Colonial Pewter, 1980. King's Dominion. Bamm-Bamm. 1.5" tall. $15-20.

Figurines, plastic. Applause, 1990. Bamm-Bamm and Pebbles are shown standing on round brown bases. 1.5" tall. $5-10 each.

Figurine, plastic. Applause, 1990. Barney is shown playing golf. 2" tall. $5-10.

Figurine, plastic. Manufacturer unknown, 1998. Dino. 3" tall. $10-15.

Figurinc, vinyl. Manufacturer unknown, 1990. Fred is shown holding a movie camera. 5.25" tall. $10-15.

Figurine, plastic. Manufacturer unknown, 1982. Fred. 2" tall. $5-10.

Figurine, vinyl. Manufacturer unknown, 1990. Dino is shown holding a bowl full of popcorn. 5.5" tall. $15-20.

Figurine, vinyl. Manufacturer unknown, 1994. Pebbles is standing on a gray base. 6.25" tall. $10-15.

Figurine, vinyl. Manufacturer unknown, 1994. Bamm-Bamm is standing on a gray base. 5.5" tall. $10-15.

CHAPTER 2
KITCHEN

Cookie jar, ceramic. Certified International Corp., 1994. Fred Flintstone is shown on a white background. Caption: "Yabba-Dabba-Doo!" 10.5" tall. $50-65.

Cookie jar, ceramic. Certified International Corp., N/A. Pebbles is shown riding on Dino's back. 13" tall. $85-100.

Cookie jar, ceramic. Manufacturer unknown, 1997. Fred is shown riding on top of a dinosaur. 11" tall. $85-100.

Salt and pepper shakers, ceramic. Certified International Corp., N/A. Fred and Barney are dressed in their Water Buffalo Lodge outfits. Under 5.25" tall. $20-35 set.

Salt and pepper shakers, ceramic. Certified International Corp., N/A. Fred is shown cooking a steak on the grill. Caption: "Kiss the cook." Under 5.25" tall. $20-35 set.

Salt and pepper shakers, ceramic. Certified International Corp., N/A. Dino is shown laying down next to his oversized food dish. Under 3.25" tall. $25-40 set.

Salt and pepper shakers, ceramic. Certified International Corp., N/A. Fred is shown sitting on top of a dinosaur at the quarry. Under 5.75" tall. $20-35 set.

Salt and pepper shakers, ceramic. Certified International Corp., N/A. Fred is shown pushing Pebbles in a stroller. Under 4.25" tall. $20-35 set.

Salt and pepper shakers, ceramic. Certified International Corp., N/A. Pebbles and Bamm-Bamm are shown standing on gray bases. Under 4" tall. $20-35 set.

Pot holder, fabric. Manufacturer unknown, 1994. Fred is shown against a polka dot background. 8.25" tall. $5-10.

Vitamins container, plastic. Bayer Corp., 1996. 100 Chewable tablets in the shape of The Flintstones characters. 4.25" tall. $5-10.

Fruit snack container, plastic. [illegible] Pan Candy, Co., 1994. Fred's hair lifts off to reveal 30 ct. of real fruit snacks. 11" tall. $10-15.

Orange drink container, aluminum. Orange Co., 1974. "Flintstones Yabba Dabba Dew." Caption: "Orange drink containing 20% orange juice." 7" tall. $20-35.

Box, plastic/paper. Kraft Foods, Inc., 1997. Package included 24 slices of American cheese and The Flintstones stickers. The back of the label has The Flintstones jokes, games, and a trivia quiz. 5.25" tall. $5-10.

Box. Nestle' USA-Food Division, Inc., 1997. Push up sherbet treats. The back of the box shows a Fred and Barney scuba activity. 7.25" tall. $5-10.

Left:
Box. Nestle' USA-Food Division, Inc., 1997. Dino Push up sherbet treats. The back of the box shows a "Rainbow finger twist" game. 7.25" tall. $10-15.

Box. Post/Kraft Foods, Inc., 1984. Fruity Pebbles brand cereal. Caption: "Play Bedrock TV Bingo." 11" tall. $20-35.

Box. Post/Kraft Foods, Inc., 1998. Fruity Pebbles brand cereal. Caption: "Free Stone Age Scrambler." 11" tall. $15-20

Box. Post/Kraft Foods, Inc., 1998. Fruity Pebbles brand cereal. Limited edition. Caption: "Bedrock Blizzard." The cereal came in frosted red and green. 11" tall. $20-35.

Box. Post/Kraft Foods, Inc., 1998. Cocoa Pebbles brand cereal. Caption: "Free Secret Sea Decoder." 11" tall. $15-20.

Molds, plastic. JELL-O promotion, 1988. The Flintstones dessert mold and instruction booklet was given out free with the purchase of packages of JELL-O brand gelatin. Fred, Barney, Pebbles, and Dino. 9.75" tall. $10-15.

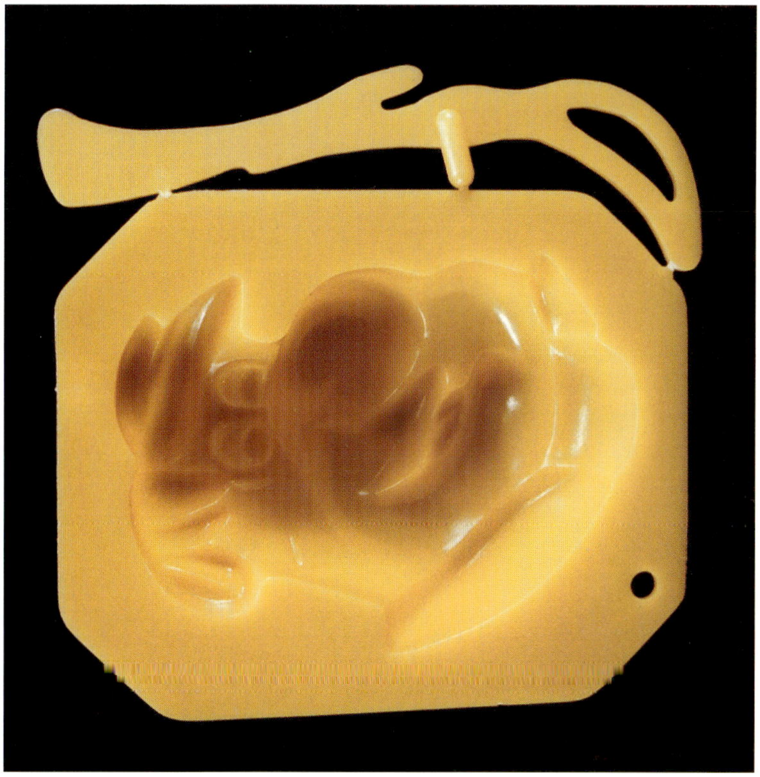

Molds, plastic. Marketplace International, 1980. Cereal premium. The handle can be broken off from the mold and then inserted into the liquid before freezing. Fred. 3" tall. $5-10.

Candy container, plastic. Pez, Inc., 1992. Fred is shown with a removable "body parts" outfit. Under 4.5" tall. $15-20.

Candy containers, plastic. Pez, Inc., 1992. Barney, Fred, Pebbles, and Dino. Under 4.5" tall. $5-10 each.

Candy container, plastic. Flix, 1995. Fred, Barney, and Pebbles contain gumballs. Under 6" tall. $5-10 each.

Candy container (top only). Bee International, 1993. Fred is shown dressed as Santa. 4" tall. $5-10.

Candy container. Flix/Willy Wonka Candy Factory, 1994. U.S.A. Fred contains "Tart-N-Tinys." 6.5" tall. $5-10.

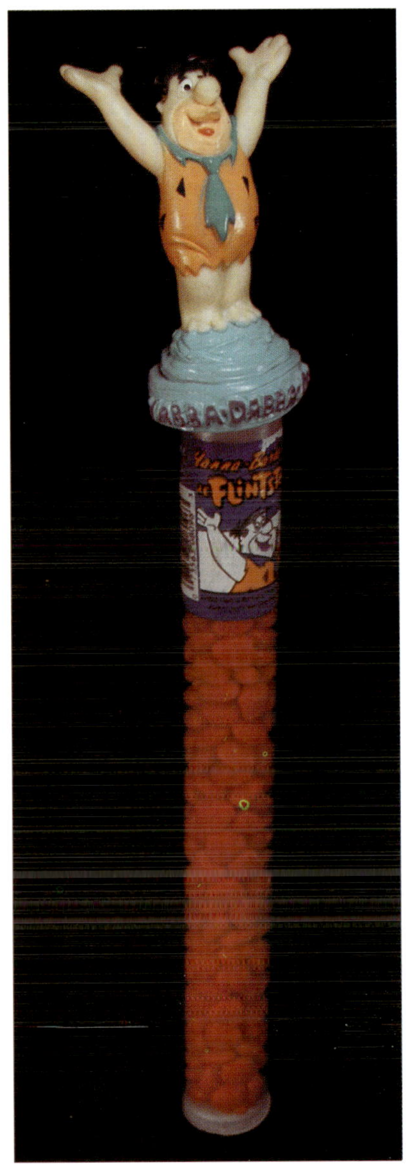

Candy container. Bee International, 1993. The top of the container can be removed to be used as a finger puppet. 13" tall. $5-10.

Candy. Bee International, 1993. Candy jewelry for Pebbles includes: a necklace, bracelet, ring, and earrings. One size. $10-15.

Napkins. Manufacturer unknown, 1969. Pebbles and Bamm-Bamm are shown riding a see-saw. One size. $10-15.

Cake decoration, plastic. Manufacturer unknown, 1973. Wilma and Pebbles are shown. 5" tall. $10-15.

Party cups, paper. C. A. Reed Co., 1964. Barney is shown holding the birthday cake. Caption: "Happy Birthday." 8 ounce hot/cold cups with handles. $15-20.

Party plates, paper. Manufacturer unknown, 1962. Barney is shown blowing out the candles on his birthday cake. 6" in diameter. $15-20.

Plate, plastic. Zak Designs, Inc., 1993. The Flintstones and Rubbles are shown having a picnic. 8" in diameter. $10-15.

Plate, plastic. Denny's promotion, 1989. The Flintstones collectors series no. 1. Caption: "Putting the cat out." 9" in diameter. $15-20.

Plate, stainless steel. Reed & Barton, 1994. Fred is shown wearing Pebbles' bowl on his head. 7" in diameter. $30-45.

Flicker magnet. Manufacturer unknown, 1991. When the magnet is moved back and forth, Fred is shown either bowling or dropping the bowling ball on his foot. 2.5" tall. $20-35.

Placemat, plastic. Denny's promotion, 1989. Fred and Barney are shown waving to Wilma and Betty. Various designs were produced. One size. $10-15.

Magnet. Magnetic Collectibles, Ltd., N/A.
Betty. Caption: "Grand Canyon, AZ." 2.75" tall.
$5-10.

Magnet. Manufacturer unknown, 1980.
Fred's head is shown. 2" tall. $5-10.

Magnet. Magnetic Collectibles, Ltd., 1994.
Betty's head is shown. 2.5" tall. $5-10.

Lunch box, plastic. Denny's Inc. promotion, 1989. Pebbles, Bamm-Bamm, and Dino are shown playing in a band. Caption: "The Flintstones. The Dinos." Lunch box: 9.5" tall. $45-60. Thermos: 6.5" tall. $15-20.

Lunch box, plastic. Denny's Inc. promotion, 1989. Bamm-Bamm is shown holding a mammoth up with one hand. Caption: "A day at the zoo." Lunch box: 9.5" tall. $45-60. Thermos: 6.5" tall, $15-20.

Baby bottles, plastic/rubber. Evenflo Products Co., 1977. Fred, Barney, and Bamm-Bamm. Under 7.5" tall. $10-15 each.

CHAPTER 3

MUGS & GLASSES

Mug, plastic. Manufacturer unknown, 1989. Caption: "The Flintstones Fruit Fizz. Fizzee Fruit Drink." 5.25" tall. $5-10.

Mug, ceramic. MSC, 1993. Fred is shown against a blue background with a bowling theme. One size. $5-10.

Mug, plastic. Deka, 1988. Caption: "Have you had your Flintstones™ brand vitamins today?" 3.75" tall. $5-10.

Mug, plastic. Manufacturer unknown, 1968. Flintstones™ brand multiple vitamins promotion. Caption: "Vitamins are good to chew." Fred. 3.25" tall. $20-35.

Mug, plastic. Manufacturer unknown, 1968. Flintstones™ brand multiple vitamins promotion. Caption: "Yabba dabba doo. Flintstones™ brand multi vitamins are good to chew." Dino. 3.75" tall. $25-40.

Mug, plastic. F & F Mold and Die works, 1972. Flintstones™ brand multiple vitamins promotion. Pebbles. 3" tall. $20-35.

Glass. Manufacturer unknown, 1977. Dino is shown knocking over some milk bottles. Caption: "The Flintstones. Bedrock City. Grand Canyon, Arizona." 5.5" tall. $25-40.

Glass. Manufacturer unknown, 1963. Caption: "The Flintstones - Pebbles' baby sitters." 4.25" tall. $15-20.

Glass. Manufacturer unknown, 1963. Caption: "The Flintstones - Fred builds a doll cave." 4.25" tall. $15-20.

Glass. Manufacturer unknown, 1962. Caption: "The Flintstones - Fred and his pal at work." 4.25" tall. $15-20.

Glass. Hardee's promotion, 1994. "The first 30 years" series. This scene is taken from the opening of each show. Caption: "Going to the Drive-in." 6" tall. $10-15.

Glass. Hardee's promotion, 1994. "The first 30 years" series. This scene is taken from when Bamm-Bamm was left in a basket on the Rubbles' door step. Caption: "Little Bamm-Bamm." 6" tall. $10-15.

Glass. Hardee's promotion, 1994. "The first 30 years" series. This scene is taken from when Fred and Barney find Dino. Caption: "The Snorkasaurus Story." 6" tall. $10-15.

Glass. Hardee's promotion, 1994. "The first 30 years" series. This scene is taken from when Pebbles was born. Caption: "The Blessed Event." 6" tall. $10-15.

CHAPTER 4
BATH

Cup holder, plastic. Hamilton Projects, Inc., 1990. The Flintstones are shown in their pajamas. 4.5" tall. $15-20.

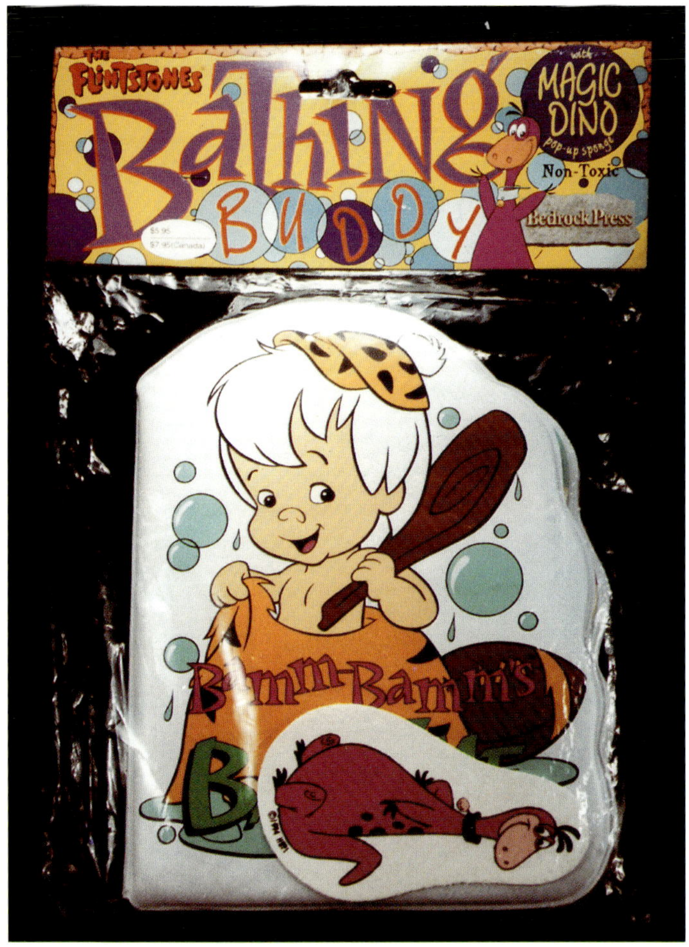

Bath sponge and book, fabric/vinyl. Turner Publishing, Inc./Bedrock Press, 1994. Titled: "Bathing buddy." 7.75" tall. $5-10.

Electric toothbrush, plastic. Kenner Products, Inc., 1974. Fred Flintstone is shown with the Flintmobile. Complete with two toothbrushes. Battery operated. 6" tall. $35-50.

Bubble bath container, plastic. Purex Corporation, Ltd., N/A. Caption: "Bamm-Bamm." 8.5" tall. $30-45.

Shampoo container, plastic. The Boots Co., 1990. England. Fred Flintstone is shown standing on a black base. 7.75" tall. $10-15.

CHAPTER 5
GENERAL HOUSEHOLD

Above: Record player, plastic. Janex Corporation, 1975. Barney is shown playing some records while Fred dances. Caption: "The Flintstones. Big Sounder." Battery operated. 9.5" tall. $150-165.

Alarm clock, metal. Manufacturer unknown, 1973. Germany. Fred Flintstone is shown wearing a red outfit. Caption: "Yabba Dabba Doo!" 7.25" tall. $60-75.

Bed ensemble, cotton/polyester. Marimac, Inc., 1991. Fred and friends are shown on sheets and pillowcases. Twin size. $20-35.

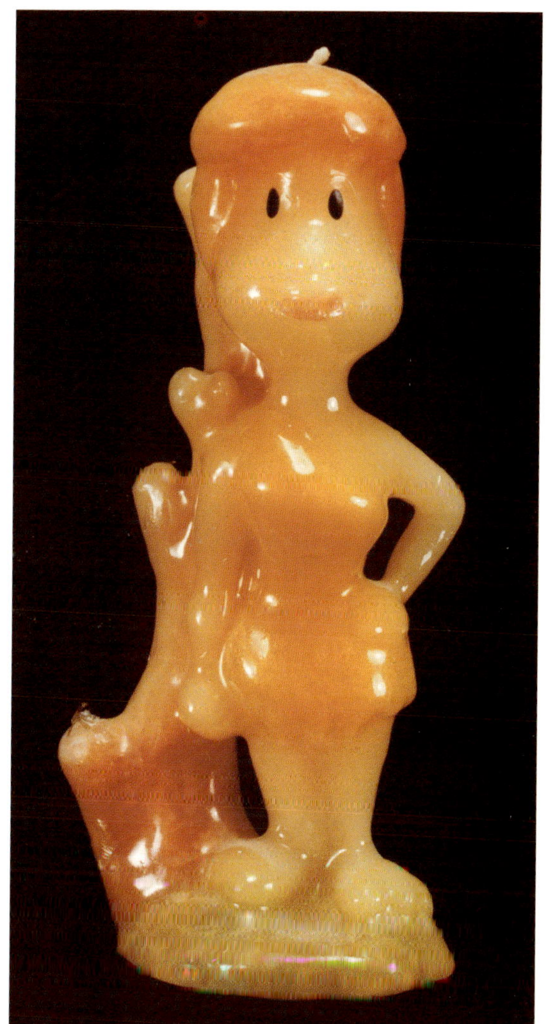

Candle. Manufacturer unknown, 1979. Wilma is shown standing next to a tree trunk. 6.25" tall. $15-20.

Nightlight, plastic. Happiness Express, Inc., 1992. Dino is shown holding Pebbles while she is sleeping. 8.5" tall. $25-40.

Lamp, plastic/fabric. Happiness Express, Inc., 1992. Dino is shown holding Pebbles while she is sleeping. The lamp shade shows silhouettes of The Flintstones characters. 13.5" tall. $50-65.

Nightlight, plastic. Manufacturer unknown, N/A. Barney. 4.25" tall. $10-15.

Nightlight, plastic. Manufacturer unknown, N/A. Fred. 4.5" tall. $10-15.

Flashlight/whistle, plastic. Gordy International, 1978. Caption: "The Flintstones whistle light." 5.25" tall. $5-10.

Print. Manufacturer unknown, N/A. Dino is shown greeting Fred at the front door. Caption: "This is to certify that this work of art has an authentic autograph acquired at the 1993 Marshfield Fair Comic Book Show on August 22, 1993." Autographed by Ray Dirgo. 17.5" tall. $250-265.

Shoe box. Manufacturer unknown, 1994.
Children's sizes. $10-15.

Frame, plastic. Brainworks, Inc., 1994. This frame can be used to enhance a computer monitor. Fred and the gang are shown at a drive-in movie. 16" tall. $15-20.

Production cell. Manufacturer unknown, N/A. Fred and Barney are shown watching a television set. Both are holding promotional merchandise from Post Fruity Pebbles cereal. This scene may have been used in a television commercial. 17.7" tall. $350-365.

Production drawing. Manufacturer unknown, N/A. Fred is shown holding two glasses of water. 10.5" tall. $50-65.

Production drawing. Manufacturer unknown, N/A. Fred. 10.5" tall. $20-35.

Poster. APC, 1979. Cereal premium. Pebbles and Bamm-Bamm are shown playing basketball. 14" tall. $5-10.

Collector plate, porcelain. Franklin Mint, 1992. Fred is shown in his car with his family and neighbors. Limited edition. For decorative use only. 8.25" in diameter. $45-60.

Sculpture, cast white metal dipped in 24K gold. Ron Lee, 1993. The Flintstones are shown in the Flintmobile. Hand painted sculpture mounted on an onyx base. Limited edition of 2750. 8.75" tall. $250-265.

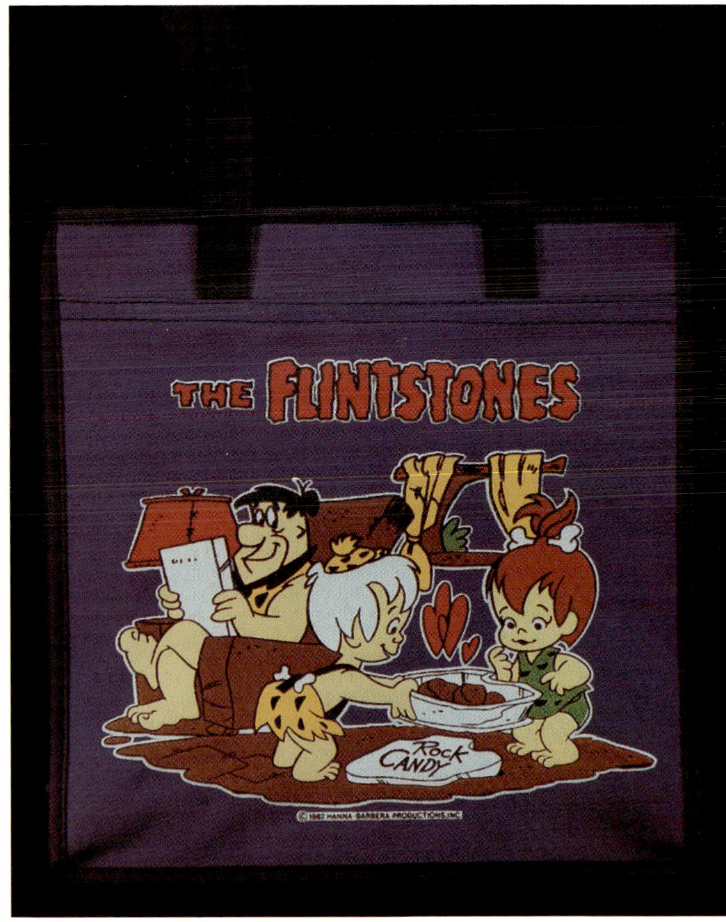

Tote bag, canvas. I.S.L. Trading Corp., 1991. Bamm-Bamm is shown giving Pebbles a piece of rock candy. 16.75" tall. $5-10.

Sculpture, resin. Hanna-Barbera Animation Art, 1996. Caption: "Creature Comforts. Barney." Barney is shown with his prehistoric hedge clipper. Limited edition of 500. 9" tall. $175-190.

Sculpture, resin. Hanna-Barbera Animation Art, 1996. Caption: "Creature Comforts. Fred." Fred is shown with his prehistoric lawn mower. Limited edition of 500. 11" tall. $225-240.

Water globe, plastic. Days Inn of America, Inc. promotion, 1994. Fred is shown driving to the Inn with his family. 3" tall. $5-10.

Change purse, plastic. Hasbro, 1975. Cereal premium. When the sides of Dino's face are pushed together, the coin slot opens in the back. 3.75" tall. $15-20

Change purse, plastic. Hasbro, 1975. Cereal premium. When the sides of Barney's face are pushed together, the coin slot opens in the back. 2.5" tall. $10-15.

Handkerchief, fabric. Manufacturer unknown, N/A. Wilma and Betty are shown waiting for Fred and Barney to come home. 11" tall. $25-40.

Iron on decal. APC, 1976. Cereal premium. Bamm-Bamm is shown driving a Stone Age racer. This was packaged with a large sticker on the reverse side. 6.5" tall. $10-15.

Handkerchief, fabric. Manufacturer unknown, N/A. Five Bedrock kids are shown playing. 11" tall. $20-35.

Patch, fabric. Voyager Emblems, Inc., 1983. Fred is shown against a white background. 2.75" in diameter. $10-15.

Flotation device, vinyl. Intex Recreation Corp., 1994. These are inflatable and can be used to assist with swimming. Children's sizes. $5-10.

Wrapping paper. American Greetings, N/A. Caption: "Yabadabadoooo, Happy Birthday to you!" Complete with two sheets. One size. $20-35.

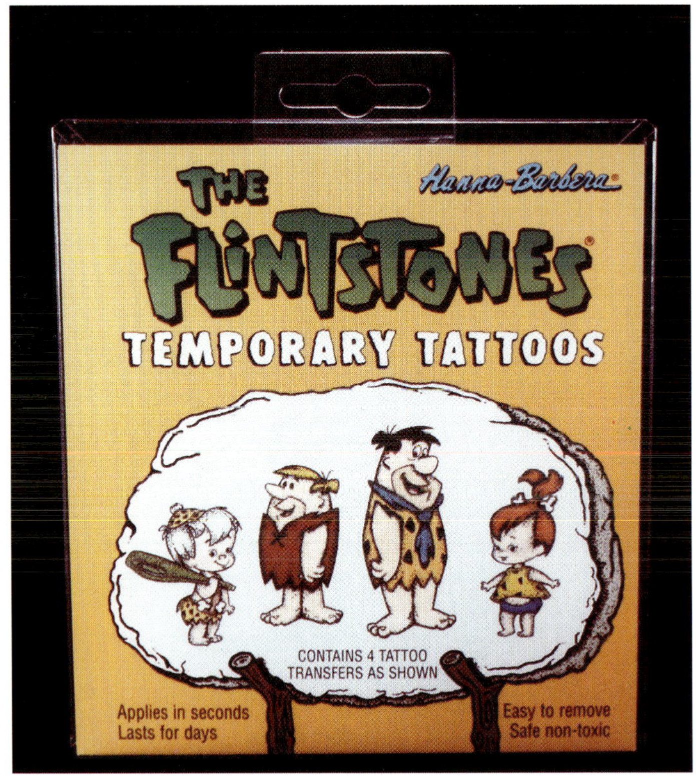

Tattoos. Highgate Products, L.L.C., 1992. Transfers of Bamm-Bamm, Barney, Fred, and Pebbles are included. 5" tall. $5-10.

Inflatable toy, vinyl. Manufacturer unknown, N/A. When Dino is squeezed, he squeaks. 23.5" tall. $35-40.

Halloween mask. Ben Cooper, Inc., 1973. Fred. Children's sizes. $45-60.

Christmas ball ornament, satin/plastic. Bradford Novelty Company, Inc., 1975. The reverse side shows Hoppy, Barney, Fred, and Pebbles. Caption: "Merry Christmas Flintstones!" 3.5" tall. $40-55.

Christmas ornament, plastic. Hallmark Cards, Inc., 1995. Betty and Wilma are shown pushing a shopping cart. 4" tall. $25-40.

Christmas ornament, plastic. Hallmark Cards, Inc., 1994. Fred and Barney are shown in the Flintmobile. 2.5" tall. $25-40.

CHAPTER 6
BANKS

Gumball bank, plastic. Hasbro, 1968. Fred Flintstone. 9" tall. $50-65.

Bank, vinyl. Manufacturer unknown, 1971. Pebbles is shown hugging Dino. 13.75" tall. $35-50.

Bank, metal. Manufacturer unknown, 1979. Fred is shown hiding a nickel from Wilma. Caption: "Bedrock Bank Unbreakable." 6.75" tall. $35-50.

Bank, vinyl. Homecraft Prod., 1973. Fred is shown in a potato sack. 8.5" tall. $45 60.

Bank, metal. Manufacturer unknown, 1979. Barney is shown holding an oversized bag of money. Caption: "Bedrock Savings & Loan. Bedrock Bank Unbreakable." 6.75" tall. $35-50.

Bank, vinyl. BBI Toys International, Ltd., 1986. Fred's head. Caption: "The Flintstones Money Bank." 5.75" tall. $15-20.

Bank, vinyl. Manufacturer unknown, 1994. Barney is shown standing on a gray base. 6.25" tall. $15-20.

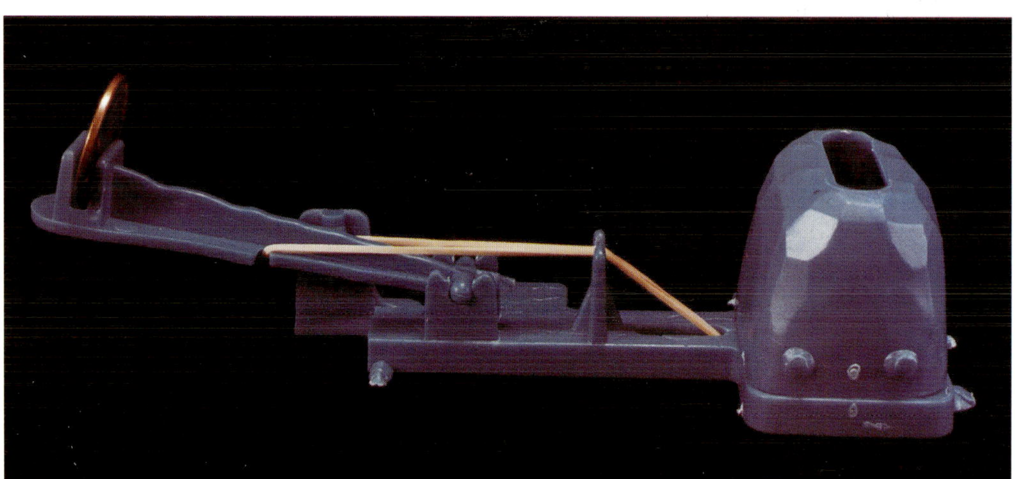

Bank, plastic. Manufacturer unknown, N/A. Cereal premium. Caption: "Rock Bank." When a coin is placed on the lever, it is thrown into the rock. 1.25" tall. $10-15.

CHAPTER 7
JEWELRY

Watch, plastic. Manufacturer unknown, 1994. Dino watch. Caption: "Modern Stone Age watches." One size. $15-20.

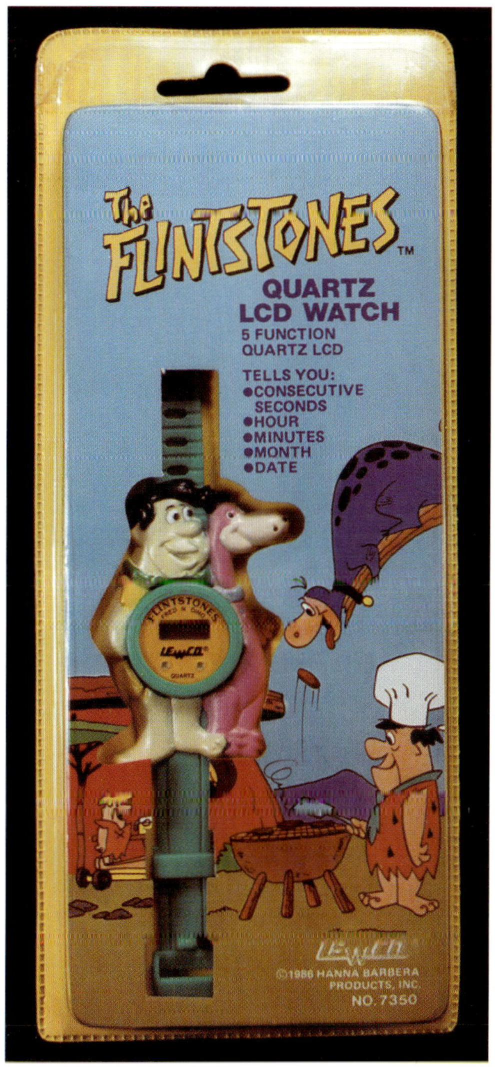

Watch, plastic. Lewco Corp., 1986. Fred and Dino are shown on a green watch band. Caption: "The Flintstones. Fred N Dino." One size. $20-35.

Watch, metal/leather. Waltham, 1994. Fred is shown bowling. Caption: "The Flintstones. Water Buffalo Lodge." One size. $45-60.

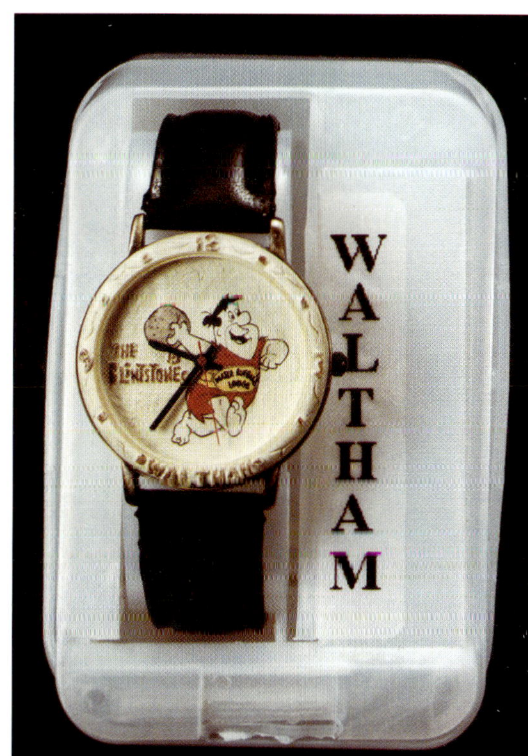

Above and right:
Watch, metal/leather. Fossil, 1993. Limited edition. "The Flintstones. Fred and Dino" collector's watch. Complete with tin lunch box and Dino pin. Lunch box: 5.5" tall. $35-50. Watch: One size. $45-60.

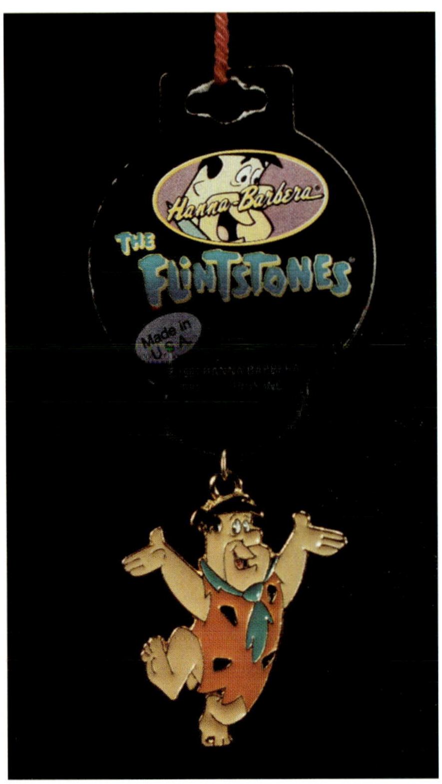

Necklaces, metal/leather. Starline, 1994. Fred. One size. $5-10.

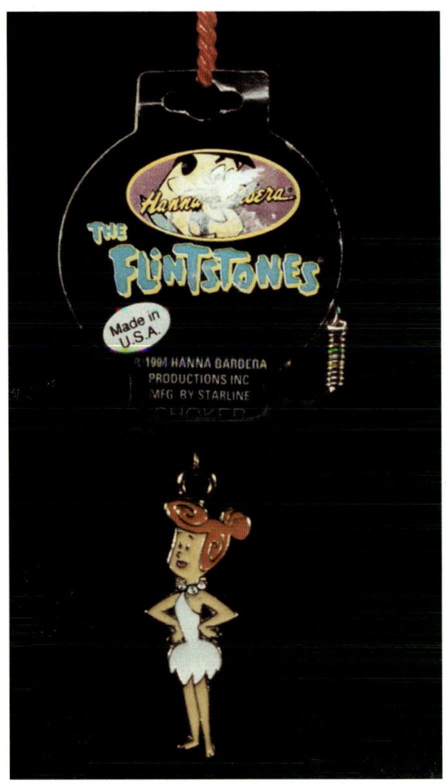

Necklaces, metal/leather. Starline, 1994. Wilma. One size. $5-10.

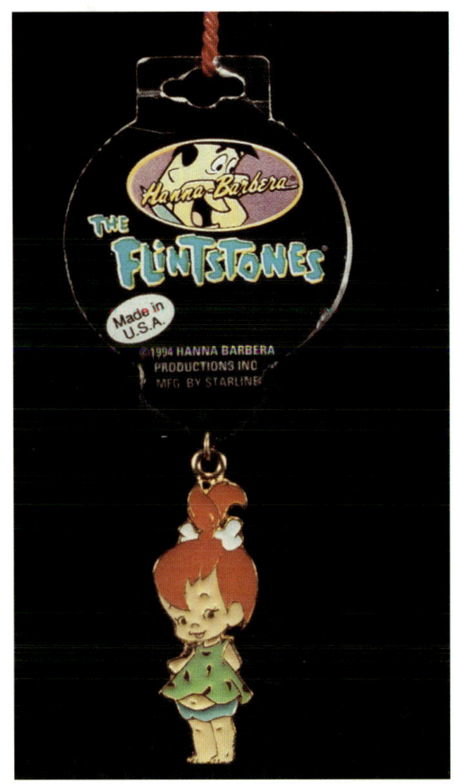

Necklaces, metal/leather. Starline, 1994. Pebbles. One size. $5-10.

Necklaces, metal/leather. Starline, 1994. Barney. One size. $5-10.

Necklaces, metal/leather. Starline, 1994. Betty. One size. $5-10.

Necklaces, metal/leather. Starline, 1994. Bamm-Bamm. One size. $5-10.

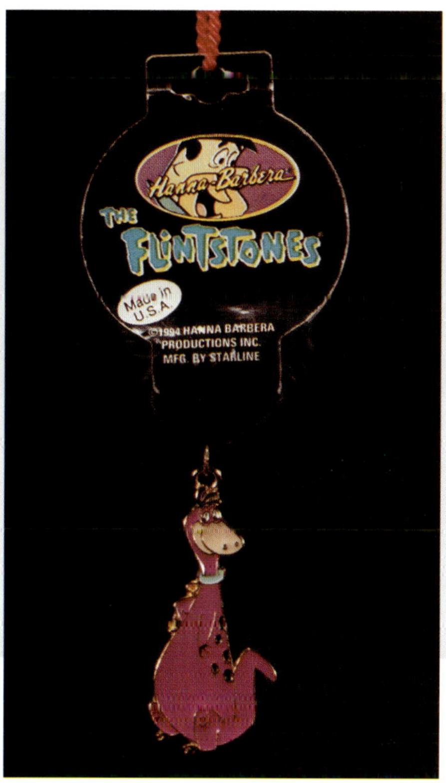

Necklaces, metal/leather. Starline, 1994. Dino. One size. $10-15.

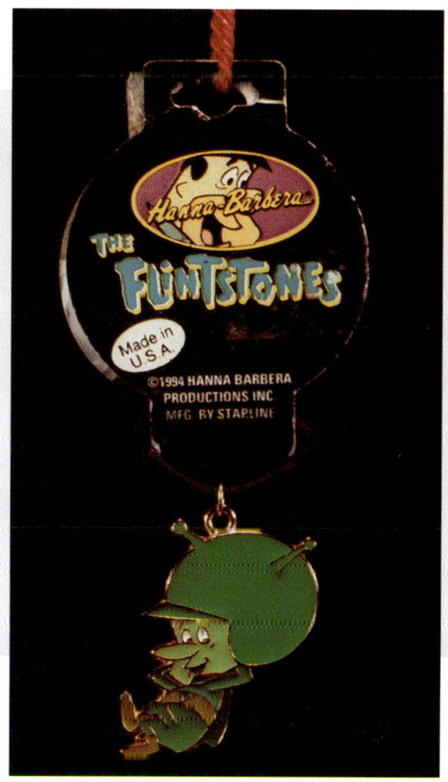

Necklaces, metal/leather. Starline, 1994. Great Gazoo. One size. $10-15.

Pin, metal. Manufacturer unknown, N/A. Universal Studios Florida promotion. 1.75" tall. $10-15.

Pin, metal. Best Seal Corp., 1982. Kings Island promotion. Fred. 3.5" in diameter. $10-15.

Pin, metal. Manufacturer unknown, N/A. Primerica Financial Services promotion. Caption: "Operation Baby Buckle." 2" tall. $15-20.

Pins, metal. Manufacturer unknown, 1973. The Flintstones, Fred, and Wilma. 0.75" in diameter. $25-40 each.

Pins, metal. Manufacturer unknown, 1973. Bamm-Bamm, Pebbles, and Barney. 0.75" in diameter. $25-40 each.

Pins, metal. Manufacturer unknown, 1973. Hoppy, Dino, and Baby Puss. 0.75" in diameter. $30-45 each.

Pins, metal. Manufacturer unknown, N/A. Fred and Barney. Caption: "Yabadabadoo." 1" in diameter. $25-40 each.

Pin, metal. Button Up, Co., 1985. Fred is shown standing against a peach background. 1.5" in diameter. $5-10.

Pin, pewter. Starline, 1994. A dinosaur shaped lawnmower is shown. 0.75" tall. $10-15.

Pin, metal. McCoy Sales Co., Inc., 1989. Fred is shown standing against a blue background. 2.5" tall. $5-10.

CHAPTER 8
TOYS

Toy, plastic/metal/fabric. A Frankonia Toy, 1962. Fred is shown playing a drum set. Caption: "Fred Flintstone's Bedrock Band." When the switch is turned on, Fred's arms and feet move up and down. Battery operated. 9.5" tall. $925-940.

Toy, plastic/metal/fabric. Louis Marx & Company, Inc., 1962. Fred is shown riding on top of Dino. Caption: "Dino the dinosaur." When the switch is turned on, Dino moves around in circles and Fred moves back and forth. Battery operated. 12.5" tall. $725-740.

Toy, plastic/metal. Louis Marx & Company, Inc., 1962. Fred is shown riding on top of Dino. Caption: "I am Dino the dinosaur. If lost, please return to Fred Flintstone." When the key on this side is wound, Dino walks in a straight line. Wind-up mechanism. 5.25" tall. $525-540.

Toy, plastic/vinyl. Azrak-Hamway International, Inc., 1974. Fred and Barney are shown driving a log car with a purple awning. When the car bumps into something, it automatically changes direction. Battery operated. 5.5" tall. $150-165.

Toy, plastic. A Child Guidance Toy, 1976. When the log shaped car is flipped, either Pebbles/Bamm-Bamm or Fred/Barney are shown driving. 5" tall. $50-65.

Toy, plastic. A Child Guidance Toy, 1976. The reverse side of log car is shown.

Toy, wood/fabric. Brio, 1962. The Flintmobile can be pulled along with the attached string. 4.25" tall. $185-200.

Toy, plastic/cardboard. Remco, 1961. Motorized sports car and trailer. Electric motor-battery operated model kit. Complete series of three. One size. $325-340.

Toy, plastic/cardboard. Remco, 1961. Motorized yacht. Electric motor-battery operated model kit. Complete series of three. One size. $325-340.

Shooting gallery game, plastic/metal. ARCO Industries, Ltd., 1976. When the key is wound, Fred, Barney, and Dino rotate around the base. Caption: "The Flintstones shooting gallery." A gun and darts were originally included, but are not shown. 9" tall. $150-165.

Toy, plastic/cardboard. Remco, 1961. A close-up of the assembled motorized yacht is shown.

Game. Transogram Company, Inc., 1961. The Flintstones Window Wacker game. Caption: "The Flintstones manor." The object of the game is to throw the balls through the plastic windows. 19.5" tall. $65-80.

Magnetic drawing kit, plastic/paper. Henry Gordy International, Inc., 1993. Caption: "The Flintstones. Wonder Wiskers." 8.75" tall. $10-15.

Drawing kit, plastic/paper. Kenner, 1984. "Draw Rings." Complete with three interlocking rings. Each ring has segments of Flintstones characters that can be traced. 11" tall. $35-50.

Drawing kit, plastic/paper. Lakeside Toys/ Lakeside Industries, 1962. Draw the Flintstones TV Show. Electric Drawing kit. Kit includes: desk, TV view sleeve, story sheets, paper, colored pencils, etc. 17.5" tall. $150-165.

An insert of the kit is shown.

Paint and crayon set. Hasbro Industries, Inc., 1973. The kit includes water color, crayons, and painting accessories. 10" tall. $35-50.

Crushed stone craft kit, cardboard/stones. A Craft Master Product of Fundimensions, 1976. The object of the craft is to texturize the cartoon background by gluing stones onto it. 13.25" tall. $35-50.

Colorforms. Colorform Brand. Titled: "The Flintstones cartoon set." The kit contains plastic pieces and a play board. 12.5" tall. $25-40.

Give-A-Show projector, plastic. Kenner Products, Co., 1963. The package included a projector and sixteen comic strip slides. Battery operated. 11" tall. $100-115.

Camera, plastic. American Far East Trading Company, Inc., 1976. Caption: "Fred Flintstone camera. Take 20 color or Black & White pictures use Kodak 126 cartridge film." 7.75" tall. $125-140.

8mm film. Screen Gems, Inc., 1963. Silent home movie. Titled: "*Dino Flintstone. Dino's Adorable.*" 3.25" in diameter. $20-35.

8mm film. Screen Gems, Inc., 1963. Silent home movie. Titled: "*The Flintstones. Golfing's Great.*" 3.25" in diameter. $15-20.

8mm film. Screen Gems, Inc., 1963. Silent home movie. Titled: "*The Flintstones. Pebbles! Daddy's Little Beauty.*" 3.25" in diameter. $15-20.

View-Master reels. View-Master/GAF Corporation, 1962. 8.25" tall. $50-65.

View-Master reels. View-Master/GAF Corporation, 1991. Titled: "The Flintstones." 8.5" tall. $15-20.

View-Master reels. View-Master/GAF Corporation, 1962. Titled: "*Los Picapiedra.*" Spanish version. 4.5" tall. $20-35.

View-Master reels. View-Master/GAF Corporation, 1964. Titled: "*The Flintstones. Pebbles and Bamm-Bamm.*" 4.5" tall. $20-35.

Game. Transogram Company, Inc. 1961. The Flintstones Stoneage game. Caption: "The game that rocked Bedrock!" One size. $50-65.

Game. Milton Bradley Company/A Division of Hasbro, Inc., 1991. The Flintstones game. Caption: "It's a Stone Age race through Bedrock." The object of the game is to be the first to gather five clams and bring Dino home. One size. $25-40.

Game. Milton Bradley Company, 1971. The Flintstones game. Fred is shown diving into a pool. The object of the game is to be the first player that can get home from vacation. One size. $25-40.

Game, plastic/cardboard. Wood Expressions, 1993. The Flintstones 3-D Chess game. Complete with 32 game pieces and game board. One size. $100-115.

Game, cardboard/glass. Whitman, 1962. The Flintstones Mitt-Full game. Complete with four cardboard characters and marbles. One size. $50-65.

Game, fabric. The Idea House, 1996. A "Big Mouth" catch game. The object of the game is to catch a Velcro ball in the mouth of either Dino or Hoppy. 11" tall. $20-35.

Roulette wheel, plastic/metal. Manufacturer unknown, 1976. Caption: "Flintstones Kelowna B.C." 3" in diameter. $15-20.

Left and far left: Fortune teller, plastic. Manufacturer unknown, 1977. Two versions, Fred or Pebbles. Each fortune teller contains a plastic character that changes shape when it is held. Each shape represents a fortune, i.e., if the sides of the character curl, it means that person is fickle. 4.25" tall. $5-10 each.

Yo-yo, tin. Manufacturer unknown, 1976. Dino is shown standing against a white background. 2.25" in diameter. $15-20.

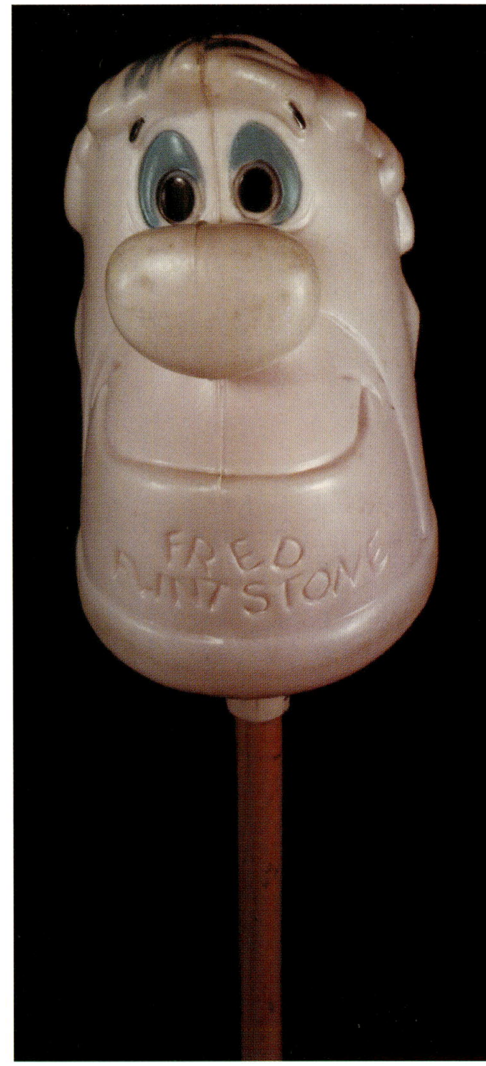

Pogo stick, plastic/wood. A. J. Renzi, 1961. The bottom of the pogo stick has a pink squeaker on it. Fred. 33.5" tall. $85-100.

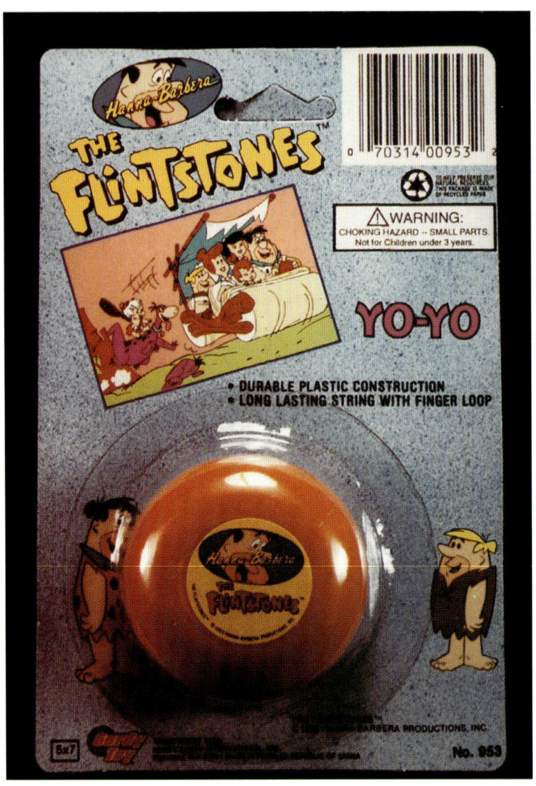

Yo-yo, plastic. Henry Gordy International, Inc., 1993. Fred is shown against an orange background. Also made in yellow. 2.25" in diameter. $5-10.

Paddle ball, wood/rubber. Manufacturer unknown, 1977. Free give-away when Bounce™, Camay™, or Mr. Clean™ was purchased. 8.75" tall. $20-35.

Tambourine, plastic/metal. Gordy International, 1978. Barney is shown playing the tambourine for Betty and Bamm-Bamm. 6" tall. $20-35.

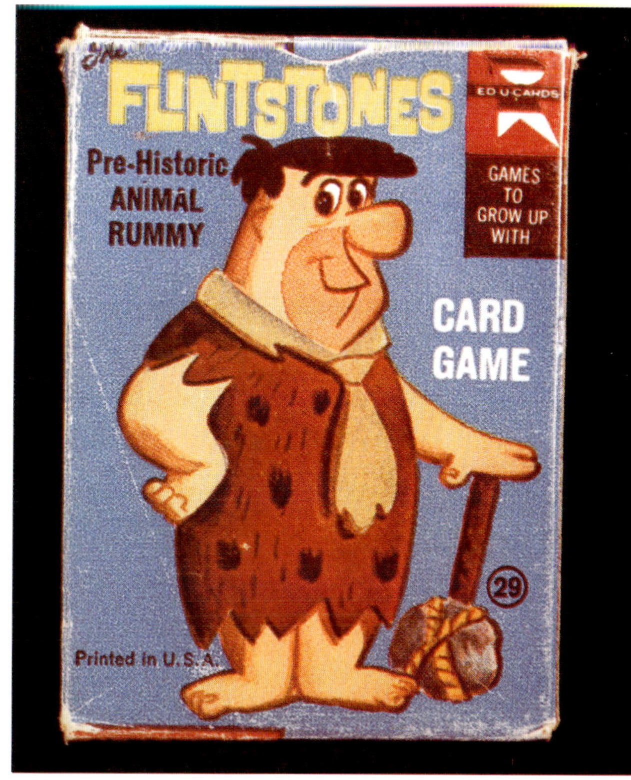

Above:
Cards. ED-U-CARDS, 1967. "Pre-Historic Animal Rummy." Complete with 35 cards. 3.75" tall. $15-20.

Far left:
Playing cards. Hoyle Products, 1979. "Fish card game." Fred and Barney are shown against a green background. 3.5" tall. $10-15.

Left:
Trading card. Primrose Conf. Company, Ltd., 1962. England. Fred and Barney are shown playing darts. Caption: "Nice throwing Barney!" 2.5" tall. $10-15.

Trading card. Cardz Distribution, Inc., 1993. The card shown was autographed by Jean VanderPyl who was the voice of Wilma and Baby Pebbles. 4" tall. Priceless.

Bowling game. Transogram, N/A. The Fred Flintstone pins originally came with three black bowling balls. (The entire set of pins is not pictured.) 5.5" tall. $5-10 each.

Bowling game, plastic/cardboard. Gag, Inc., N/A. Cereal premium. The kit included ten bowling pins and one plastic bowling ball. Under 2.75" tall. $20-35.

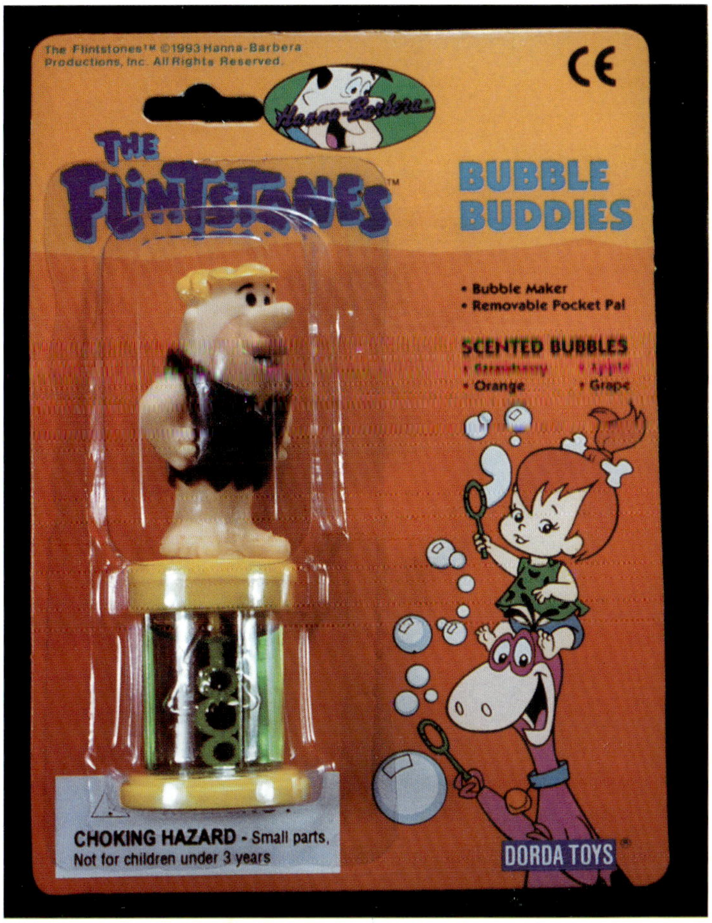

Bubble toy, vinyl/plastic. Dorda Toys, 1993. "Bubble Buddies" series. Complete set of eight. Barney. Under 4.5" tall. $5-10.

Bubble toy, vinyl/plastic. Dorda Toys, 1993. "Bubble Buddies" series. Complete set of eight. Bamm-Bamm. Under 4.5" tall. $5-10.

Bubble toy, vinyl/plastic. Dorda Toys, 1993. "Bubble Buddies" series. Complete set of eight. Betty. Under 4.5" tall. $5-10.

Frisbee, plastic. Manufacturer unknown, 1984. Cereal premium. Barney. 3.5" in diameter. $5-10.

Roll toy, plastic. JVC Company, N/A. Cereal premium. There is a silver ball underneath that glides Wilma when she is pushed. 1.25" tall. $15-20.

Toy, plastic. Manufacturer unknown, N/A. Cereal premium. Caption: "Grabbers." When the handle of the grabber is pressed together, the end can be used to pick up things. Fred. 3" tall. $10-15.

Bicycle reflector, plastic. W. G. Inc., N/A. Cereal premium. Fred. 3.5" tall. $5-10.

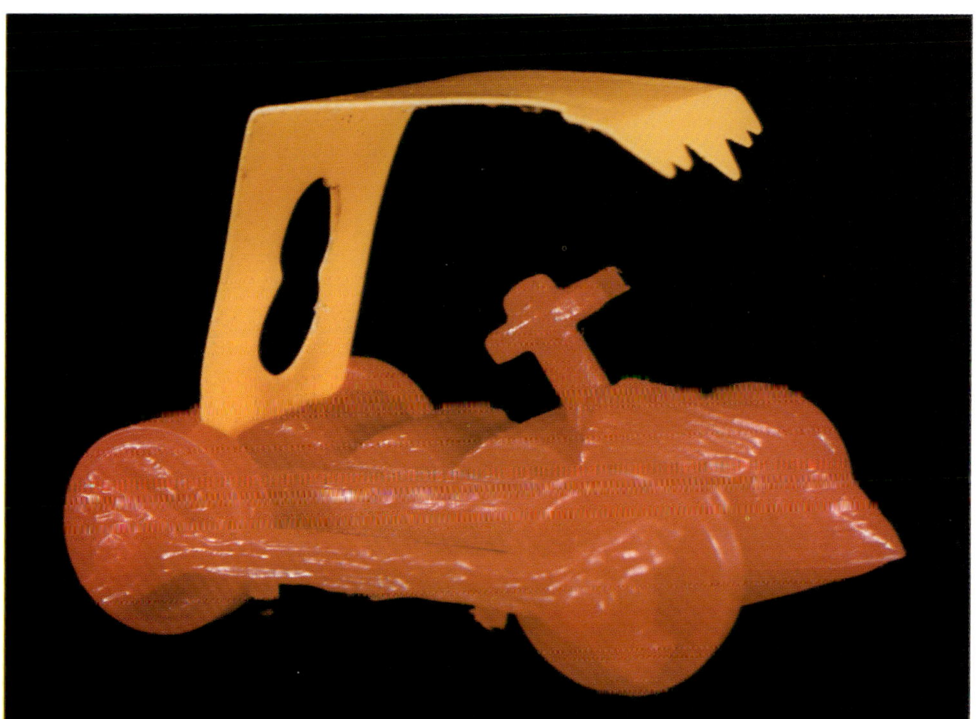

Toy, plastic/poly film. JVC Co., 1970. Cereal premium. The Rubble's log car. 1.75" tall. $15-20.

Toy, plastic. Manufacturer unknown, 1990. Cereal premium. Fred Flintstone's car is shown with one big wheel in the center. 1.5" tall. $5-10.

Toy, plastic. Manufacturer unknown, N/A. Cereal premium. Fred is shown riding on top of a dinosaur at the quarry. 1.75" tall. $20-35.

Toy, plastic. W.G., Inc., N/A. Cereal premium. "The Flintstones Land/Sea Vehicle." This vehicle is complete with a winding stick and break mechanism. Under 2.5" tall. $15-20.

Toy, plastic/poly film. Toy Development Co., 1972. "Flintmobile Car" promotion from Flintstones™ Brand Multiple Vitamins. Original cost was $0.75 plus a picture of Fred from the vitamin package. This car is powered by a motor that is run on a rubber band. 3.25" tall. $35-50.

Toy, metal, Hot Wheels, 1994. Titled: "The Flintstones Flintmobile." When the car is submerged in warm water, it changes color. 1.5" tall. $20-35.

Toy, metal/plastic. Corgi, 1982. Fred is shown in an orange car. 1.5" tall. $20-35.

Toy, metal. Action Performance Companies, Inc., 1996. Officially licensed Winston Cup collectible. A yellow car decorated with The Flintstones characters is shown. Complete with a limited edition collectors card. 1" tall. $20-35.

Toy, plastic. Applause, 1990. Fred is shown driving his car. 2" tall. $10-15.

Toy, metal. Racing Champions, Inc., 1996. Officially licensed Winston Cup collectible. A yellow car decorated with The Flintstones characters is shown. Mounted on a black base. 4.75" tall. $35-50.

Ramp Walker, plastic. Marx Toys, 1962. When string is tied to the loop in front, Fred and Barney can be pulled so that they walk in unison. 2.75" tall. $135-150.

Walker, vinyl/plastic. Boley Corporation, 1992. Fruity Pebbles cereal promotion. Mail ordered through Bedrock shop free Stone Age stuff offer. Fred and Barney. Wind-up. 3" tall. $15-20 each.

Walker, plastic. Manufacturer unknown, 1993. Pebbles is shown in a baby walker. Wind-up. 4" tall. $15-20.

Toy, plastic. Kohner Bros., Inc., 1967. Caption: "Tricky Trapeze. Push Button Acrobat." Fred spins around the bar when the buttons are pressed on the base. 5.75" tall. $65-80.

Spin toy, plastic. Kohner Brothers, Inc., N/A. Caption: "Spinkin." When the string on the base is pulled, Fred revolves. 4.5" tall. $50-65.

Push-up puppet, plastic. Kohner Brothers, Inc., N/A. Bamm-Bamm is shown holding a club. When the button underneath the base is pushed, Bamm-Bamm moves around. 3.75" tall. $35-50.

Push-up puppet, plastic. Kohner Brothers, Inc., N/A. Pebbles is shown holding a red block. When the button underneath the base is pushed, Pebbles moves around. 3.75" tall. $35-50.

Author's note: If the label on the base of an acrobat, spinkin, or push-up puppet is missing, the value drops dramatically.

Push-up puppet, plastic. Arco Industries, Ltd., 1976. Fred is shown wearing a blue tie. 4.5" tall. $35-50.

Hand puppet, vinyl/fabric. Knickerbocker Toy, Co., 1962. Barney is shown with green hair. 9" tall. $65-80.

Loft:
Finger puppet, vinyl. Knickerbocker Toy, Co., 1972. Bamm-Bamm is shown holding a green club. 3" tall. $10-15.

Right:
Action figure, plastic. D-Toys S.A./Irwin Toy, Ltd., 1983. Spain. Fred's arms, legs, and head are moveable. 3.5" tall. $20-35.

Action figure, plastic. D-Toys S.A./Irwin Toy, Ltd., 1985. Spain. Wilma's arms, legs, and head are moveable. Complete with two garden tools. 4" tall. $20-35.

Action figure, plastic. D-Toys S.A./Irwin Toy, Ltd., 1983. Spain. Barney's arms, legs, and head are moveable. Complete with one golf bag, one strap, and two golf clubs. 2.75" tall. $20-35.

Action figure, plastic. D-Toys S.A./Irwin Toy, Ltd., 1985. Spain. Betty's arms, legs, and head are moveable. Complete with two garden tools. 3.75" tall. $20-35.

Action figures, plastic. D-Toys S.A./Irwin Toy, Ltd., 1983. Spain. Pebbles and Bamm-Bamm. Their arms, legs, and heads are moveable. Complete with one club. Under 2.5" tall. $20-35 each.

Toy, plastic. Denny's promotion, 1990. "The Flintstones Vehicles" series. Complete set of six. Wilma is shown in a gray car. Under 2" tall. $5-10.

Toy, plastic. Denny's promotion, 1990. "The Flintstones Vehicles" series. Complete set of six. Fred is shown in the Flintmobile. Under 2" tall. $5-10.

Toy, plastic. Denny's promotion, 1990. "The Flintstones Vehicles" series. Complete set of six. Barney is shown in a log car. Under 2" tall. $5-10.

Toy, plastic. Denny's promotion, 1990. "The Flintstones Vehicles" series. Complete set of six. Pebbles is shown in a dinosaur car. Under 2" tall. $5-10.

Toy, plastic. Denny's promotion, 1990. "The Flintstones Glacier Gliders" series. Complete set of six. Fred is shown on ice skates. 2.75" tall. $5-10.

Toy, plastic. Denny's promotion, 1990. "The Flintstones Vehicles" series. Complete set of six. Dino is shown in a gray wagon. Under 2" tall. $10-15.

Toy, plastic. Denny's promotion, 1990. "The Flintstones Glacier Gliders" series. Complete set of six. Bamm-Bamm is shown on a toboggan. 1.5" tall. $5-10.

Toy, plastic. Denny's promotion, 1990. "The Flintstones Glacier Gliders" series. Complete set of six. Pebbles is shown on a saucer sled. 2" tall. $5-10.

Toy, plastic. Denny's promotion, 1990. "The Flintstones Glacier Gliders" series. Complete set of six. Barney is shown on ice skates. 2.5" tall. $5-10.

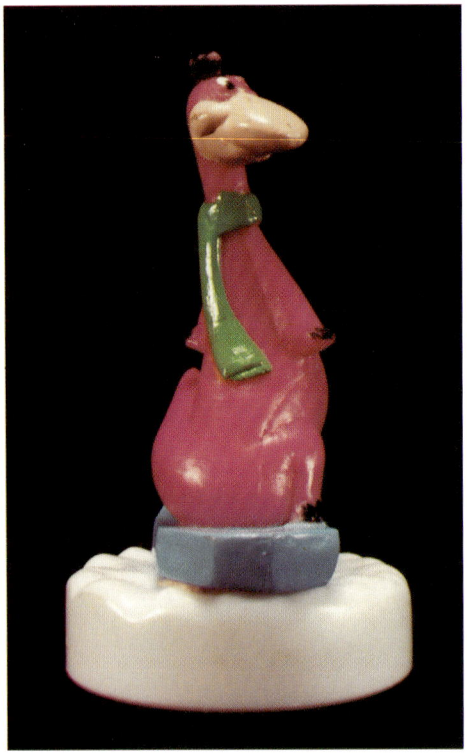

Toy, plastic. Denny's promotion, 1990. "The Flintstones Glacier Gliders" series. Dino is shown on a blue snowboard. Complete set of six. 2.75" tall. $10-15.

Toy, plastic. Denny's promotion, 1990. "The Flintstones Glacier Gliders" series. Complete set of six. Hoppy is shown on skis. 2.5" tall. $10-15.

Toy, plastic. Denny's promotion, 1991. "The Flintstones Dino-Racers" series. Complete set of six. Fred is shown riding on top of a green dinosaur. 2.25" tall. $5-10.

Toy, plastic. Denny's promotion, 1991. "The Flintstones Dino-Racers" series. Complete set of six. Dino is shown riding on top of a gray dinosaur. 2.25" tall. $10-15.

Toy, plastic. Denny's promotion, 1991. "The Flintstones Dino-Racers" series. Complete set of six. Pebbles is shown riding on top of a blue dinosaur. 2.25" tall. $5-10.

Toy, plastic. Denny's promotion, 1991. "The Flintstones Dino-Racers" series. Complete set of six. Barney is shown riding on top of a purple dinosaur. 2.25" tall. $5-10.

Toy, plastic. Denny's promotion, 1991. "The Flintstones Dino-Racers" series. Complete set of six. Betty is shown riding on top of a blue dinosaur. 2.25" tall. $5-10.

Toy, plastic. Denny's promotion, 1991. "The Flintstones Dino-Racers" series. Complete set of six. Bamm-Bamm is shown riding on top of a green dinosaur. 2.25" tall. $5-10.

Toy, vinyl. Denny' s promotion, 1991. "The Flintstones Fun Squirters" series. Complete set of six. Fred, Pebbles, and Wilma. 2.5" tall. $5-10 each.

Toy, vinyl. Denny's promotion, 1991. "The Flintstones Fun Squirters" series. Complete set of six. Dino, Bamm-Bamm, and Barney. 2.5" tall. $5-10 each.

Toy, plastic. Denny's promotion, 1991. "The Flintstones Stone Age Cruisers" series. Complete set of six. Fred is shown in a blue vehicle. 3" tall. $5-10.

Toy, plastic. Denny's promotion, 1991. "The Flintstones Stone Age Cruisers" series. Complete set of six. Wilma is shown in a red vehicle. 3" tall. $5-10.

Toy, plastic. Denny's promotion, 1991. "The Flintstones Stone Age Cruisers" series. Complete set of six. Pebbles is shown on a pink Pteranodon. 3" tall. $5-10.

Toy, plastic. Denny's promotion, 1991. "The Flintstones Stone Age Cruisers" series. Complete set of six. Dino is shown in a boat. 3" tall. $10-15.

Toy, plastic. Denny's promotion, 1991. "The Flintstones Stone Age Cruisers" series. Complete set of six. Barney is shown in a yellow motorcycle. 3" tall. $5-10.

Toy, plastic. Denny's promotion, 1991. "The Flintstones Stone Age Cruisers" series. Complete set of six. Bamm-Bamm is shown in an orange vehicle. 3" tall. $5-10.

Toy, plastic. Denny's promotion, 1991. "The Flintstones Rock & Rollers" series. Complete set of six. Pebbles is shown playing a tambourine. 2.5" tall. $5-10.

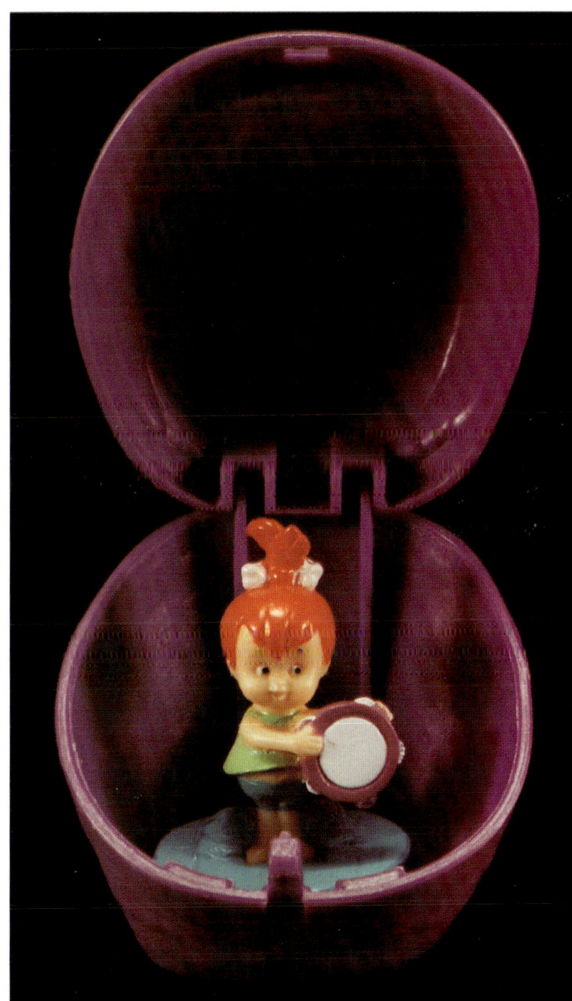

Toy, plastic. Denny's promotion, 1991. "The Flintstones Rock & Rollers" series. Complete set of six. Fred is shown playing a guitar. 2.5" tall. $5-10.

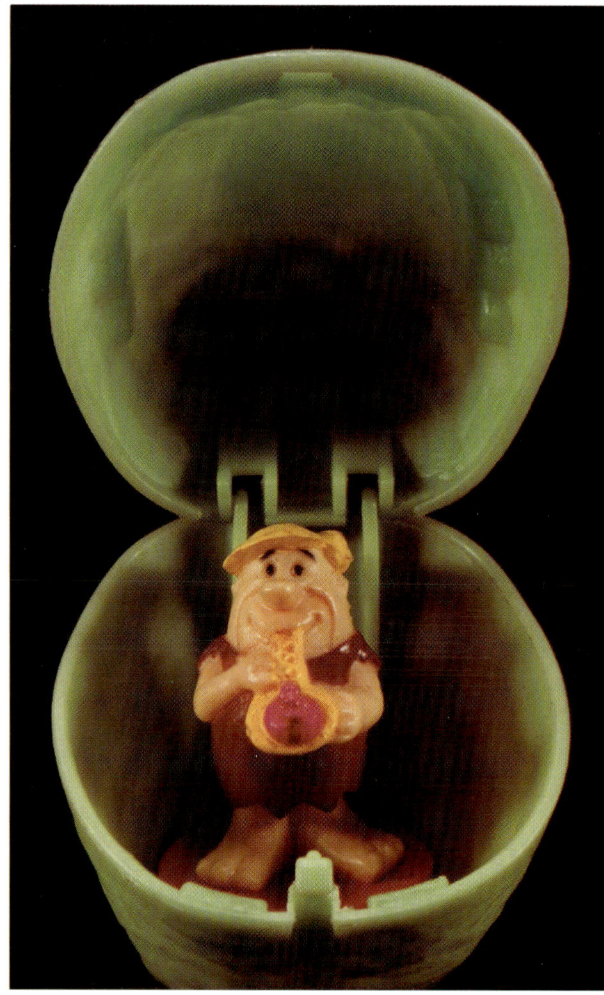

Toy, plastic. Denny's promotion, 1991. "The Flintstones Rock & Rollers" series. Complete set of six. Dino is shown playing the keyboard. 2.5" tall. $10-15.

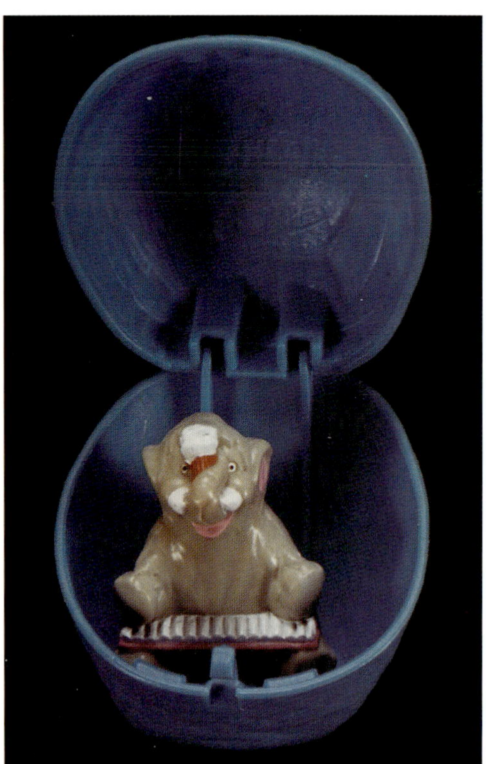

Above:
Toy, plastic. Denny' s promotion, 1991. "The Flintstones Rock & Rollers" series. Complete set of six. Barney is shown playing the saxophone. 2.5" tall. $5-10.

Far left:
Toy, plastic. Denny' s promotion, 1991. "The Flintstones Rock & Rollers" series. Complete set of six. Mammoth is shown playing the keyboard. 2.5" tall. $10-15.

Left:
Toy, plastic. Denny' s promotion, 1991. "The Flintstones Rock & Rollers" series. Complete set of six. Bamm-Bamm is shown playing the drums. 2.5" tall. $5-10.

Toy, vinyl. Manufacturer unknown, 1995. Dino is shown on a surfboard. 1.5" tall. $10-15.

Toy, plastic. Subway promotion. Johnson Grossfield, Inc., N/A. Fred is shown driving the Flintmobile. 2.75" tall. $5-10.

Toy, plastic. Burger King promotion, 1997. "Wacky Racers" series. Dino is shown holding his hands over Fred's eyes. 2.5" tall. $10-15.

Toy, plastic. Dairy Queen promotion, 1997. Barney is shown playing the drums. 2.5" tall. $10-15.

Toy, plastic. Dairy Queen promotion, 1997. Wilma is shown playing the keyboard. 2.75" tall. $10-15.

Toy, plastic. Dairy Queen promotion, 1997. Fred is shown holding a microphone. 3" tall. $10-15.

Toy, plastic. Dairy Queen promotion, 1997. Dino is shown playing the tambourine. 3" tall. $15-20.

CHAPTER 9
PUZZLES

Above left:
Puzzle, plastic/cardboard. Manufacturer unknown, 1990. Fred is shown against a geometric background. 3.5" tall. $5-10.

Above:
Puzzle, plastic/cardboard. Manufacturer unknown, 1990. Barney is shown against a geometric background. 3.5" tall. $5-10.

Left:
Slide puzzle, plastic. Manufacturer unknown, N/A. The puzzle pieces slide to reflect images of Fred, Betty, Wilma, and Barney. 2.5" tall. $110-115.

Puzzle, paper. Manufacturer unknown, 1997. Cereal premium. "Stone Age Scrambler" series. The puzzle can be folded to show six different scenes. One size. $10-15.

Puzzle, wood. Manufacturer unknown, N/A. Fred is shown lying in a hammock. 9 pieces. $25-40.

Puzzle, cardboard. Manufacturer unknown, 1980. Cereal premium. Wilma on roller skates. The reverse side shows a picture of Bamm-Bamm playing baseball. 6 pieces. 4" tall. $10-15.

Puzzle, cardboard. Manufacturer unknown, 1980. Cereal premium. Betty playing tennis. The reverse side shows a picture of Fred in his pajamas. 6 pieces. 4" tall. $10-15.

Puzzle. Whitman Publishing Company (UK) Limited, 1973. Fred, Wilma, Barney, and Betty are shown dancing in front of a band. 63 pieces. $40-55.

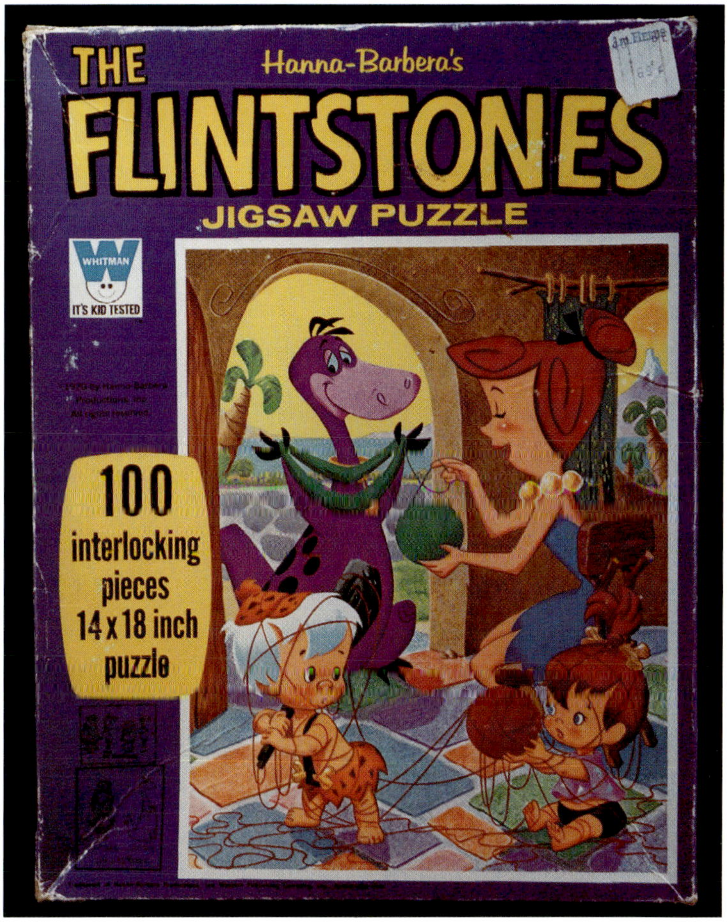

Puzzle. Whitman/Western Publishing Company, Inc., 1970. Wilma, Bamm-Bamm, Pebbles, and Dino are shown with balls of yarn. 100 pieces. $15-20.

Puzzle, cardboard. Milton Bradley Company, 1991. Pebbles, Dino, and Bamm-Bamm are shown playing on the beach. 60 pieces. $5-10.

Puzzle. Milton Bradley Company, 1991. Fred is shown with his family at the "Mr. Rib" drive-thru. 60 pieces. $5-10.

Puzzle. Whitman/Western Publishing Company, Inc., 1968. Fred and Barney are shown standing next to a sailboat. 99 pieces. $15-20.

Puzzle, cardboard. Whitman Publishing Company, 1960. Frame-tray puzzle. Fred and Dino are shown golfing. 48 pieces. $25-40.

Puzzle, cardboard. Whitman Publishing Company, 1962. Frame-tray puzzle. Barney and Betty are shown dancing. 16 pieces. $20-35.

Puzzle, cardboard. Whitman Publishing Company, 1964. Frame-tray puzzle. Pebbles and Bamm-Bamm are shown playing with a turtle. 19 pieces. $20-35.

Puzzle, cardboard. Whitman Publishing Company, 1964. Frame-tray puzzle. Pebbles and Bamm-Bamm are shown playing with Baby Puss. 37 pieces. $25-40.

CHAPTER 10
DOLLS & PLUSH

Paper dolls. Manufacturer unknown, 1976. "T.V. Character Stand-ups." One size. $20-35.

Paper dolls. Whitman Publishing Company, 1964. Bamm-Bamm is shown holding Pebbles up in the air. Complete with two dolls, two stands, 55 outfits, and one pair of plastic scissors. 15.5" tall. $65-80.

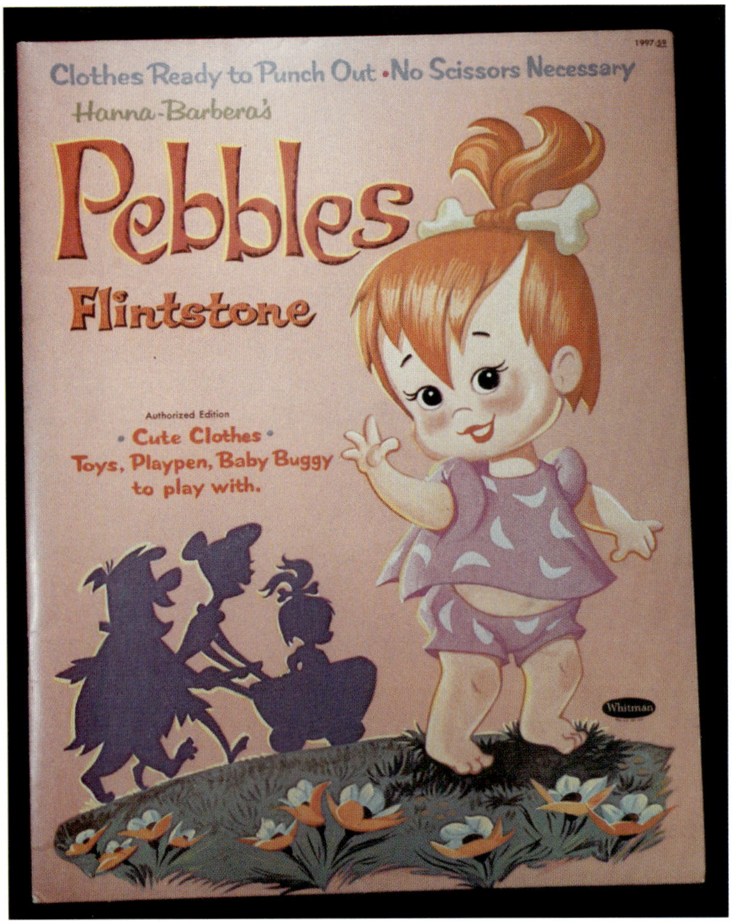

Paper dolls. Whitman Publishing Company, 1963. Pebbles Flintstone punch-out paper doll with clothes, toys, playpen, and a baby buggy. 13" tall. $40-65.

Paper dolls. Wonder Books/Grosset & Dunlap, Inc., 1974. Betty and Barney punch-out paper dolls with various outfits. 11.5" tall. $20-35.

Paper dolls. Wonder Books/Grosset & Dunlap, Inc., 1974. Pebbles and Dino punch-out paper dolls with various outfits. 11.5" tall. $20-35.

Paper dolls. Wonder Books/Grosset & Dunlap, Inc., 1974. Pebbles & Bamm-Bamm punch-out paper dolls with various outfits. 11.5" tall. $20-35.

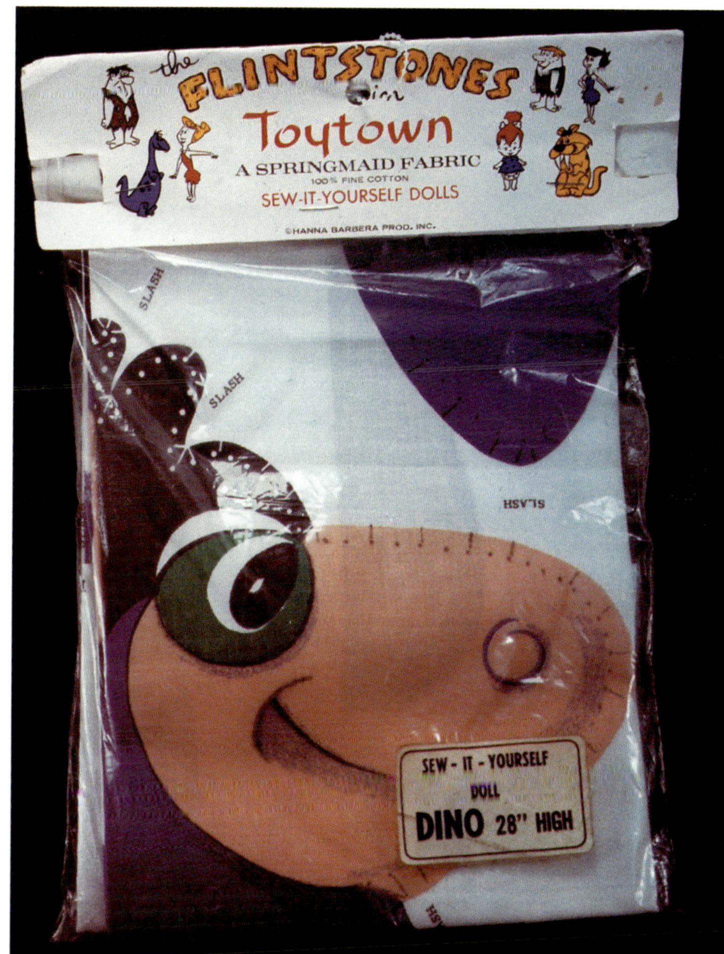

Cloth doll. Manufacturer unknown, N/A. Dino "sew-it-yourself" doll. One size. $45-70.

Cloth doll. Manufacturer unknown, N/A. Pebbles "sew-it-yourself" doll. One size. $40-65.

Doll, plastic/fabric. Ideal Toy Corporation, N/A. Bamm-Bamm is shown wearing a yellow printed outfit. The doll decreases in value if he is not complete with the original bone, club, and hat. 12" tall. $150-165.

Doll, plastic/fabric. Ideal Toy Corporation, 1965. Pebbles is shown wearing a tan printed shirt and black shorts. The doll decreases in value if she is not complete with the original bone in her hair. 8.5" tall. $150-165.

Doll, vinyl. Manufacturer unknown, 1960. Barney is shown with green hair. 10" tall. $85-100.

Doll, vinyl. Manufacturer unknown, 1960. Baby Puss. 10" tall. $225-240.

Doll, vinyl. R. Dakin & Co., 1970. Pebbles. 7.75" tall. $35-50.

Doll, vinyl. R. Dakin & Co., 1970. Barney. 7" tall. $35-50.

Dolls, plastic/plush. Shottman International, Inc., 1989. Denny's promotion. Fred and Wilma. Each character has a molded loop in its head. Complete set of eight. Less than 4" tall. $5-10 each.

Doll, vinyl. R. Dakin & Co., 1970. Bamm-Bamm. A club was originally included, but is not shown. 7" tall. $35-50.

Dolls, plastic/plush. Shottman International, Inc., 1989. Denny's promotion. Pebbles, Betty, and Bamm-Bamm. Each character has a molded loop in its head. Complete set of eight. Less than 4" tall. $5-10 each.

Left:
Doll, vinyl. Kenner Productions, N/A. Pebbles. 6" tall. $15-20.

Right:
Doll, vinyl. Manufacturer unknown, 1980. Barney's head, arms, and legs are moveable. 5.75" tall. $15-20.

Below left:
Doll, vinyl. Kenner Productions, N/A. Bamm-Bamm is shown sucking his thumb. 5.75" tall. $15-20.

Below right:
Doll, vinyl/plush. Strottman International, Inc., 1994. Days Inn promotion. The Flintstones "Travel Buddies" series. Fred. 9" tall. $20-35.

Doll, vinyl/plush. Strottman International, Inc., 1994. Days Inn promotion. The Flintstones "Travel Buddies" series. Pebbles. 6.25" tall. $20-35.

Doll, vinyl/plush. Applause, Inc., 1990. Fred Flintstone. 13" tall. $20-35.

Dolls, vinyl/fabric. Knickerbocker Toy Company, Inc., 1973. Pebbles, Bamm-Bamm, and Barney. 4" tall. $10-15 each.

Doll, vinyl/plush. Applause, Inc., 1990. Pebbles. Caption: "The Yabba-dabba-doo Crew." 13" tall. $20-35.

Plush. Nanco, 1990. Pebbles is shown with fuzzy hair. 10.5" tall. $10-15.

Plush. Canasa Trading Corp., 1987. Fred is shown with fuzzy hair. 10.25" tall. $10-15.

Plush. Nanco, 1990. Bamm-Bamm is shown with fuzzy hair. 16.5" tall. $10-15.

Plush. Nanco, 1989. Fred is shown holding a Christmas gift. 11" tall. $20-35.

Plush. Play-By-Play, 1993. Barney. 6.75" tall. $10-15.

Plush. Nanco, 1989. Barney is shown holding a Christmas gift. 11" tall. $20-35.

Plush. Strottman International, 1988. Cereal premium. This toy came attached to the top of a cereal box. Dino. 4.75" tall. $10-15.

Plush. Play-By-Play, 1993. Dino is shown with felt accents. 8" tall. $15-20.

Plush. Mighty Star, 1980. Dino is shown wearing a collar with a yellow tag. 9" tall. $15-20.

Plush. Play-By-Play, 1994. Dino is shown wearing a white sport shirt. Caption: "Panthers 85." 8.5" tall. $20-35.

CHAPTER 11
STATIONERY

Stamper, plastic/rubber. Cereal premium, 1993. Fred is shown with a star in the background. Caption: "Hollyrock." 1.5" in diameter. $5-10.

Stamper, plastic. Taco Bell promotion, 1995. Dino is shown on a green dinosaur. The bottom can be removed to reveal a concealed ink pad. 2.25" tall. $15-20.

Stamper, plastic. Taco Bell promotion, 1995. Fred is shown on a blue golf cart. The bottom can be removed to reveal a concealed ink pad. 2.25" tall. $10-15.

Floaty pens. Manufacturer unknown, 1994. Denmark. The reverse side shows The Flintstones characters either playing baseball or bowling. When the pen is tipped, the ball floats from one end to the other. 6" tall. $20-35 each.

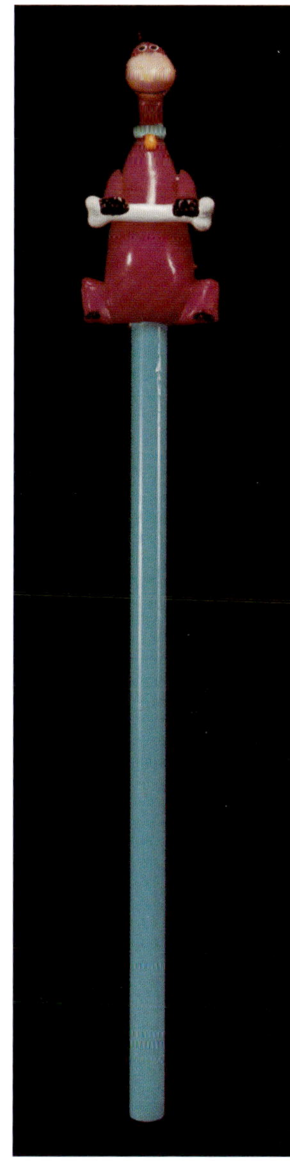

Pencil. Applause, 1990. When the lever is pushed on Dino's back, his arms move up and down. 9" tall. $10-15.

Pencil holder, plastic. GPI, Inc., 1974. Cereal premium. Dino's tail can hold a pencil. 3" tall. $5-10.

Calendar, plastic/paper. Bermas L.I.C., 1979. Cereal premium. Caption: "Calendar caddy." The position of the paper cube can be changed to reflect the date. The bottom edge of the caddy has a ruler on it. 3.25" tall. $10-15.

Chalk. Advance Crayon & Color, Corp., 1962. Complete with 16 white and colored chalks. 4" tall. $30-45.

Postcard. Facet Publishers, 1964. Fred is shown playing a "Stoneway" piano. Barney is shown playing a drum labeled "Fred Flintstone Band." 4" tall. $10-15.

Postcard. Manufacturer unknown, 1966.
Holland. Fred and Barney are shown fishing.
4" tall. $10-15.

Postcard. Manufacturer unknown, 1964.
Holland. Fred is shown taking a bath in a
tortoise shell. 4" tall. $10-15.

Postcard. Manufacturer unknown, 1964. Holland. Wilma and Fred are shown cleaning their house. 4" tall. $10-15.

Stickers. Manufacturer unknown, N/A. Cereal premium. Pebbles. 3" tall. $5-10.

Stickers. Manufacturer unknown, N/A. Cereal premium. Barney. 3" tall. $5-10.

Stickers. Gibson Greetings, Inc., 1990. Dino is shown in various poses. Removable. 2 sheets. 7.5" tall. $5-10.

Sticker. APC, 1976. Cereal premium. Barney is shown in the bath tub. This was originally packaged with a large iron-on patch on the reverse side. 6.5" tall. $10-15.

Stickers. Manufacturer unknown, 1977. Three dimensional stickers of The Flintstones. 16.5" tall. $20-35.

Sticker. Manufacturer unknown, 1981. Fred. Caption: "Kings Island." 5.25" tall. $10-15.

Sticker. Manufacturer unknown, 1982. Wilma. 5.25" tall. $5-10.

Sticker. Manufacturer unknown, 1982. Dino. 5.25" tall. $10-15.

Sticker. Manufacturer unknown, 1980. Barney. 5" tall. $5-10.

CHAPTER 12
BOOKS, RECORDS, & VIDEO

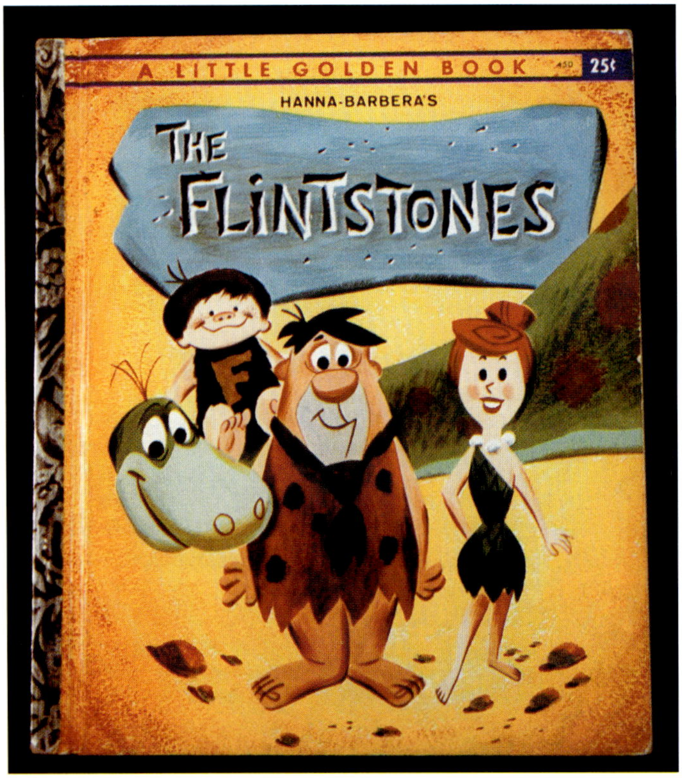

Hardcover book. Golden Press, Inc., 1960. A Little Golden Book. *The Flintstones* by Mel Crawford. 8" tall. This book is very desirable because it mentions two obscure characters. One is a child named "Junior" and the other is a dinosaur pup named "Harvey." These characters may have been the predecessors of Pebbles and Dino. 8" tall. $20-35.

Hardcover book. Golden Press, Inc., 1963. A Little Golden Book. *Bamm-Bamm with Pebbles Flintstone* by Jean Lewis. Pictures by Hawley Pratt and Norm McGary. 8" tall. $10-15.

Hardcover book. World Distributors (Manchester), Ltd. (UK); under the arrangement of Ottenheimer Publishers, Inc., 1974. 3-D Pop-up book. *The Flintstones and the Unhappy Rich Man*. Author unknown. 7.75" tall. $20-35.

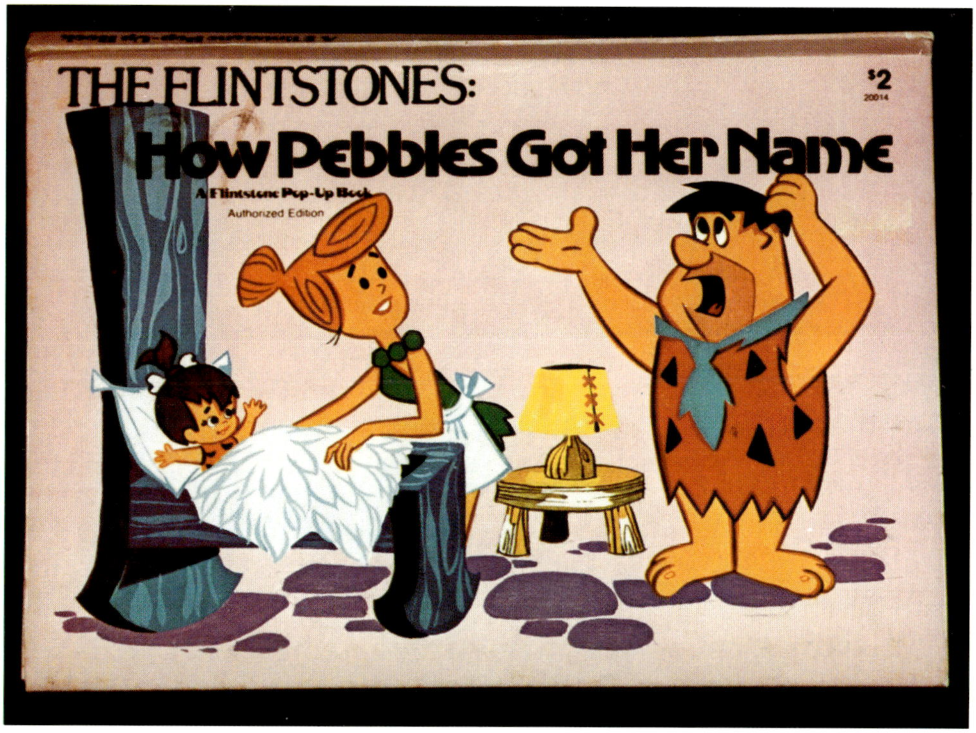

Hardcover book. World Distributors (Manchester), Ltd. (UK); under the arrangement of Ottenheimer Publishers, Inc., 1974. 3-D Pop-up book. *The Flintstones: How Pebbles Got Her Name*. Author unknown. 7.75" tall. $20-35.

Hardcover book. Turner Publishing, Inc., 1995. A Pull-n-Peek™ Opposites Book. *The Flintstones: Big Race in Bedrock* by Leslie McGuire. Designed by Willabel L. Tong. Pencils by Iwao Takamoto. Paints by Vaccan Associates, Inc., Pat Keppler. 6.5" tall. $10-15.

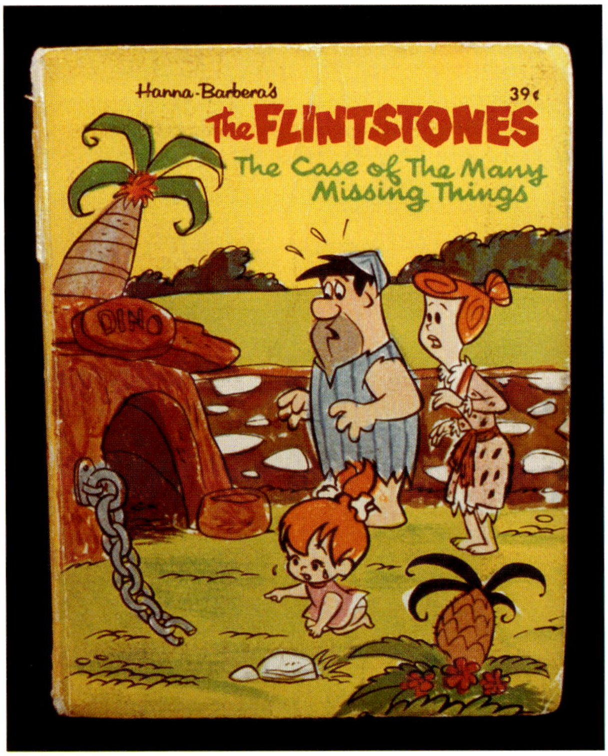

Hardcover book. Western Publishing Company, Inc., 1968. A Big Little Book. *The Flintstones: The Case of the Many Missing Things* by Paul S. Newman. 5" tall. $20-35.

Softcover book. Ottenheimer Publishers, Inc., 1977. *The Flintstones: A friend from the Past* by Horace J. Elias. 4.5" tall. $15-20.

Hardcover book. Western Publishing Company, Inc., 1964. A Whitman Tell-A-Tale Book. *Pebbles Flintstone: Daddy's Little Helper* by Patrick Hagen. Illustrated by Robert Storms. 6.5" tall. $15-20.

Softcover book. Ottenheimer Publishers, Inc., 1972. *The Flintstones: on a Picnic with Dino* by Horace J. Elias. 7.25" tall. $10-15.

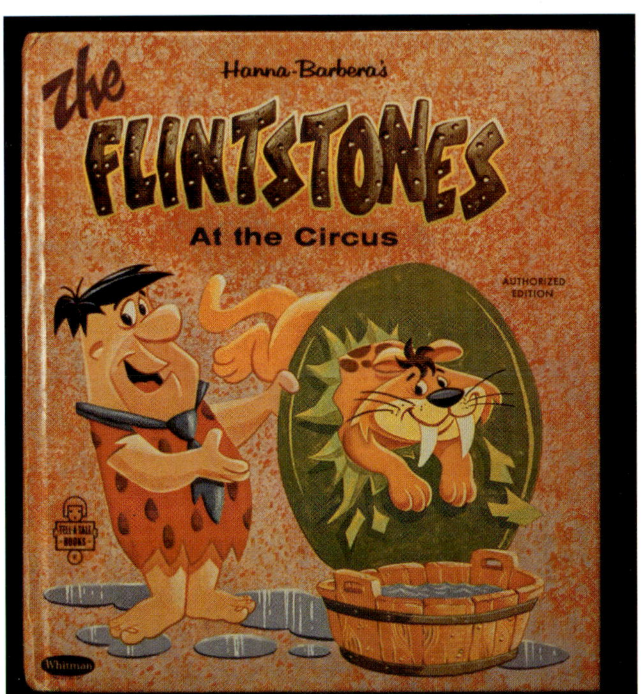

Hardcover book. Western Publishing Company, Inc., 1963. A Whitman Tell-A-Tale Book. *The Flintstones: At the Circus* by Jean Lewis. Illustrated by Frank McSavage and Robert Heiner. 6.5" tall. $15-20.

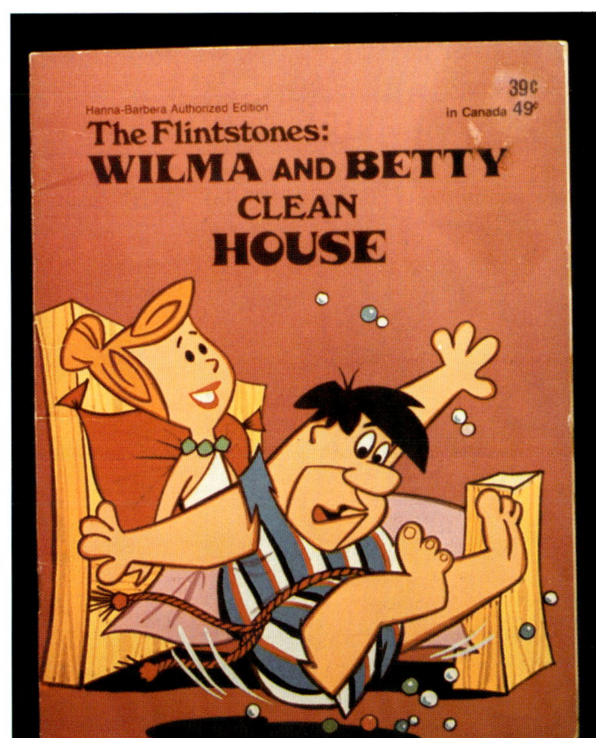

Softcover book. Ottenheimer Publishers, Inc., 1974. *The Flintstones: Wilma and Betty Clean House* by Horace J. Elias. 8" tall. $10-15.

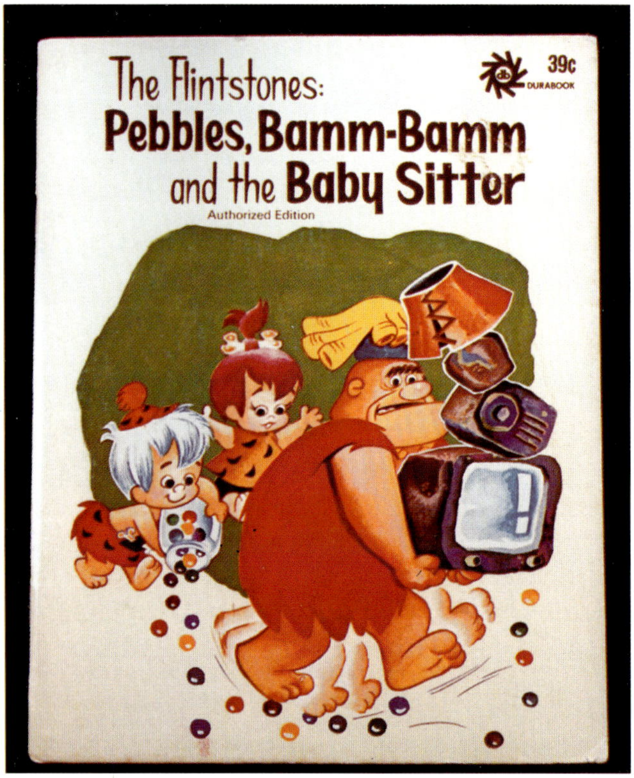

Left:
Softcover book. Modern Promotions, 1972. *The Flintstones: Pebbles, Bamm-Bamm and the Baby Sitter* by Horace J. Elias. 8" tall. $15-20.

Softcover book. Ottenheimer Publishers, Inc., 1979. *The Flintstones: Dino Finds A Goldmine* by Horace J. Elias. 7" tall. $10-15.

Softcover book. Ottenheimer Publishers, Inc., 1978. Author unknown. *The Flintstones: The Mystery of Mammoth Mansion*. 7" tall. $5-10.

Softcover book. Ottenheimer Publishers, Inc., 1978. *Pebbles and Bamm-Bamm and the Wicked Witch* by Mark Evanier. 7" tall. $5-10.

Softcover book. Ottenheimer Publishers, Inc., 1982. *Pebbles & Bamm-Bamm: The Jelly Bean Mine* by Horace J. Elias. 7" tall. $5-10.

Softcover dictionary. Spindex Corporation, 1979. *Thumb Ease The Flintstones Dictionary*. The definitions in the dictionary are illustrated with The Flintstones characters. 6" tall. $10-15.

Author's note: This out-of-print book is an excellent resource for The Flintstones history and trivia.

Hardcover book. Turner Publishing, Inc., 1994. *The Flintstones: A Modern Stone Age Phenomenon* by T. R. Adams. 11.25" tall. $30-45.

Activity book. Ottenheimer Publishers, Inc, 1978. Author unknown. *Fred and Barney's Crazy Mixed-Up Mazes*. 7.75" tall. $5-10.

Activity pad. Landoll, Inc., 1994. Fred and Dino are shown standing side by side. 8" tall. $5-10.

Activity pad. Landoll, Inc., 1994. Pebbles and Bamm-Bamm are shown playing with Dino. 7.75" tall. $5-10.

Coloring and Activity book. Landoll, Inc., 1997. Fred is shown with his family and friends. 10.5" tall. $10-15.

Coloring and Activity book. Landoll, Inc., 1994. Dino is shown licking Fred's face. 14" tall. $10-15.

Coloring book. Modern Promotions a division of Unisystems, Inc., 1976. *The Flintstones Present Carrot Capers*. 14" tall. $15-20.

Comic book. K. K. Publications, Inc., January 1963. Gold Key series. *The Flintstones*. Captions: "Fred is out to win the great Stone Age hot rod race" and "Introducing the Rubbles' new bundle of noise." 10" tall. $20-35.

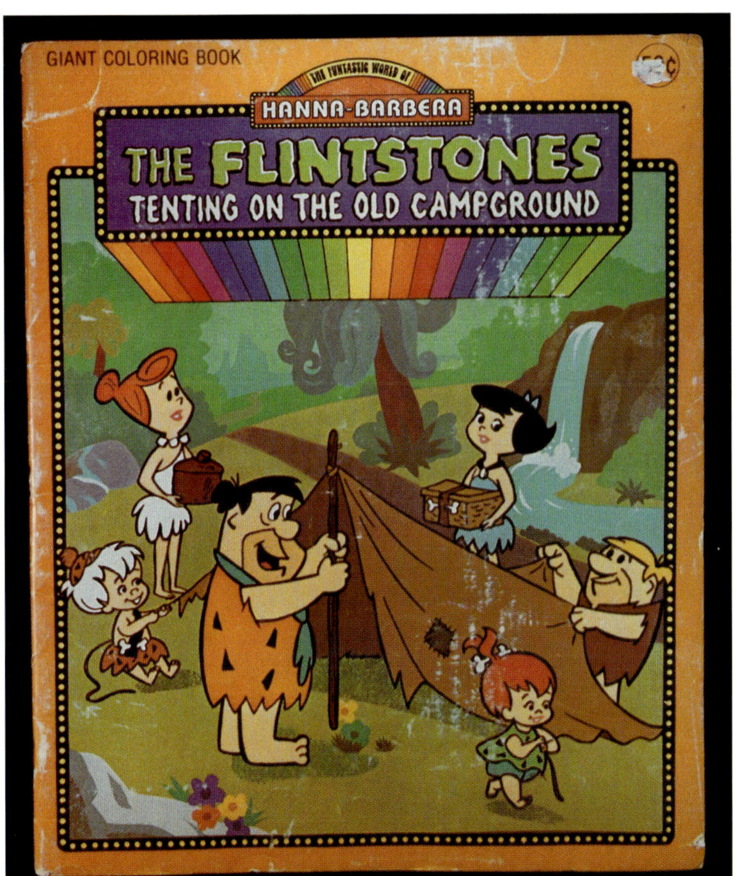

Coloring book. Modern Promotions a division of Unisystems, Inc., 1977. *The Flintstones: Tenting on the Old Campground*. 14" tall. $15-20.

Comic book. K. K. Publications, Inc., January 1965. Gold Key series. *The Flintstones with Pebbles and Bamm-Bamm.* 10" tall. $10-15.

Comic book. K. K. Publications, Inc., September 1964. Gold Key series. *The Flintstones Meet the Gruesomes with Pebbles and Bamm-Bamm.* 10" tall. $20-35.

Comic book. Blackthorne Publishing, Inc., February 1988. *The Flintstones 3-D.* Fred, Wilma, and Pebbles are shown looking at a photo album. 10.25" tall. $20-35.

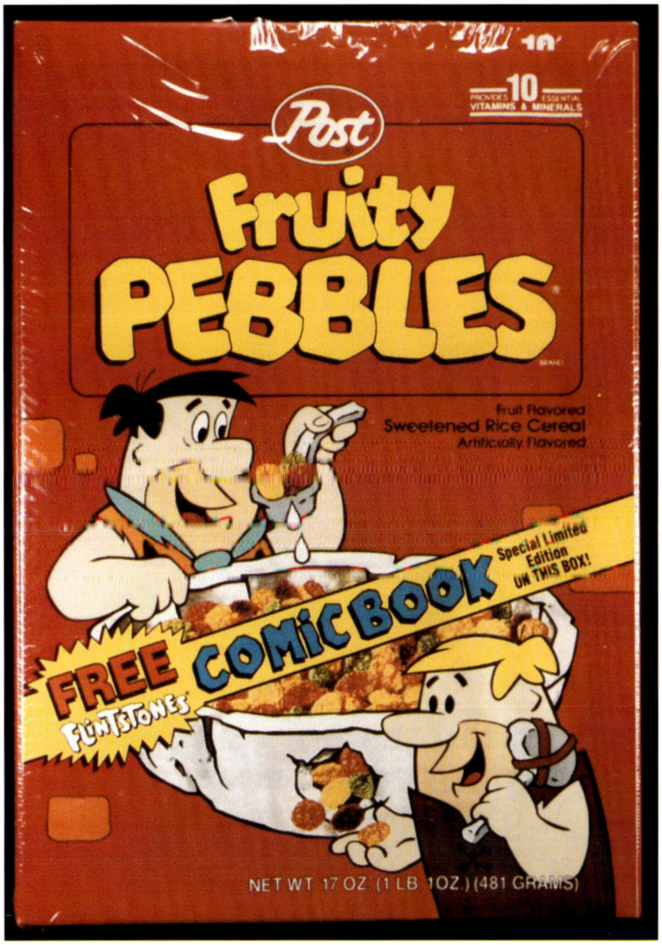

Comic book. Manufacturer unknown, 1993. Cereal premium. *Fruity Pebbles™*. *Free Flintstones Comic Book*. The comic book was shrink wrapped directly to the cereal box. It's cover reflected the same artwork as on the cereal box. 11.5" tall. $15-20.

Book/record. Peter Pan Industries, 1976. *Fred Flintstone and Good, Old, Unreliable Dino*. 7.25" tall. $15-20.

Activity book/record. Hearseedo/Baker Rhodes Marketing, Corp., 1973. *Hanna-Barbera Record of Safety*. Wilma is shown driving with Pebbles and Dino. Complete with record, coloring book, and poster. 12.25" tall. $35-50.

Book/record. Peter Pan Industries, 1981. *Fred Flintstone the Magician.* 7.25" tall. $10-15.

Book/record. Peter Pan Industries, 1981. *Fred & Barney in Circus Fun.* 7.25" tall. $10-15.

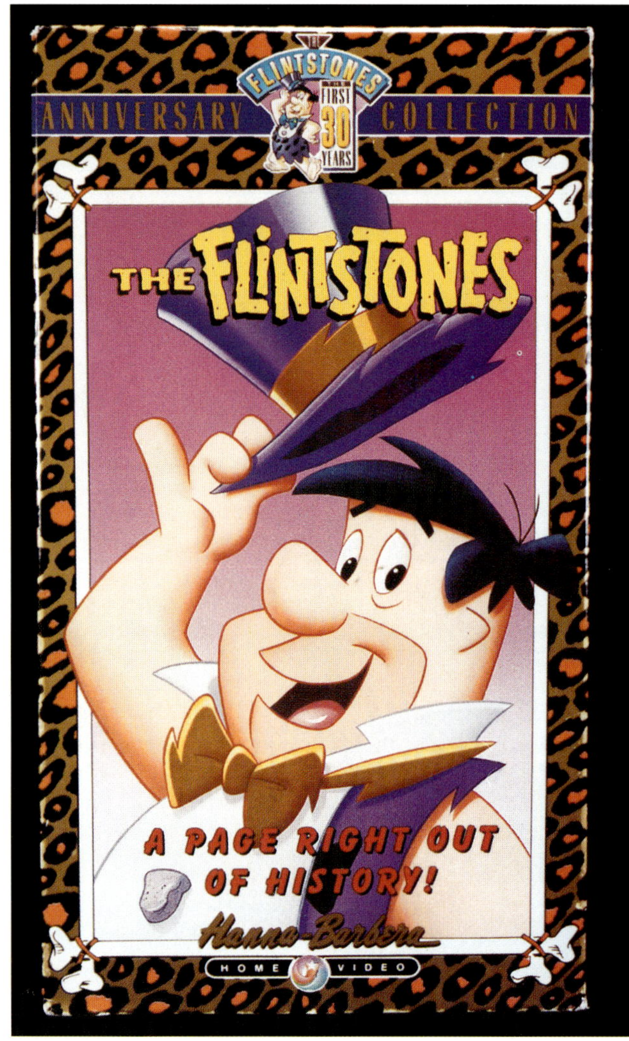

Video. Hanna-Barbera Home Video, 1981. *The Flintstones. A Page Right Out of History.* This video was produced to commemorate The Flintstones 30th anniversary. It includes the episode when Pebbles was born. VHS. $15-20.

BIBLIOGRAPHY

Adams, T.R. *The Flintstones, A Modern Stone Age Phenomenon*. Atlanta, Georgia: Turner Publishing, Inc., 1994.

Aikins, Larry. *Vinyl and Plastic Lunch Boxes*. Gas City, Indiana: L-W Book Sales, 1992.

Gagliasso, Dan. *Collecting Toys Magazine*. Waukesha, WI: Kalmbach Publishing Co., August 1997.

Korbeck, Sharon. *Toy Shop Magazine*. Iola, Wisconsin: Krause Publications, Bi-Weekly Distribution 1998-1999.

Longest, David. *Cartoon Toys and Collectibles*. Paducah, Kentucky: Collector Books, 1999.

Pope, Gail, and Hammond, Keith. *Fast Food Toys*. Atglen, Pennsylvania: Schiffer Publishing, Ltd., 1996

Reed, Robert. *Toy Collector and Price Guide Magazine*. Iola, Wisconsin: Krause Publications, October 1995.

Solomon, Charles. *The History of Animation Enchanted Drawings*. Avenel, New Jersey: Wong Books-Distributed by Random House Value Publishing Inc., 1989, 1994.

Stulb, Vickie. *Modern Banks*. Gas City, Indiana: L-W Book Sales, 1997.

The Flintstones. A Page Right Out of History. Hanna-Barbera Home Video, 1981.

Woodall, Allen, and Brickell, Sean. *The Illustrated Encyclopedia of Metal Lunch boxes*. Atglen, Pennsylvania: Schiffer Publishing, Ltd., 1992.

WWW.SCHIFFERBOOKS.COM

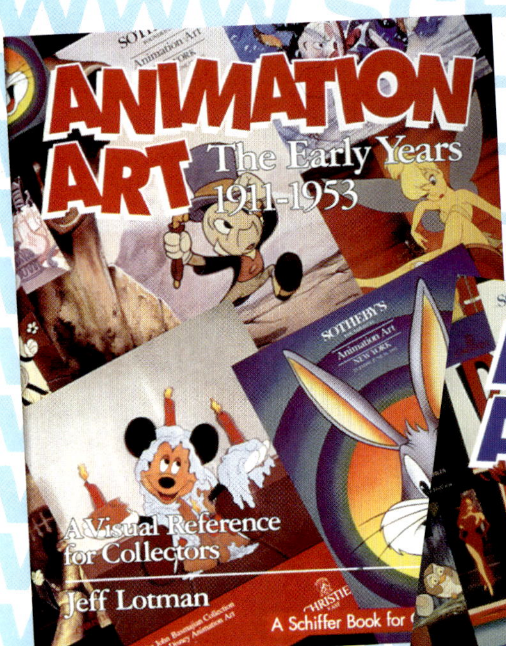

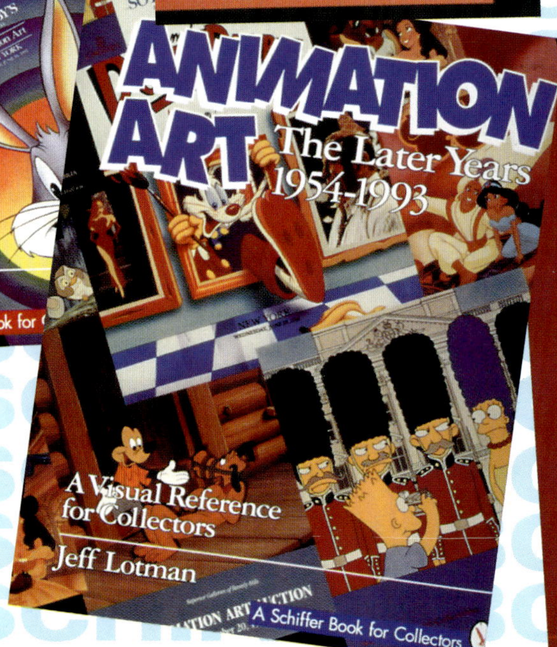